De Gaulle

De Gaulle
Philippe Masson

Editor-in-Chief: Barrie Pitt
Editor: David Mason
Art Director: Sarah Kingham
Picture Editor: Robert Hunt
Consultant Art Editor: Denis Piper
Designer: Barry Miles
Illustration: John Batchelor
Photographic Research: Jonathan Moore
Cartographer: Richard Natkiel

Photographs for this book were especially selected from the following Archives: left to right pages 4-5 Imperial War Museum; 8 Keystone Press Agency; 10 Samedi-Soir; 11 Keystone; 12 Rene Dazy; 13 US National Archives; 14 Camera Press/IWM; 14 Popperphoto; 16 US Archives; 17 Keystone; 18 IWM; 20 US Archives; 22 H Roger Viollet; 23 Fox Photos; 24 US Archives; 26 Keystone; 27-8 US Archives; 30-1 IWM; 32 Keystone; 33 Popper; 34 Camera; 36-7 US Archives; 39 Popper; 40 Viollet; 41 Keystone; 41-2 US Archives; 43-4 Keystone; 45 Archive du Comite d'Histoire de la Seconde Guerre Mondial; 46 IWM; 48 Photo Service de Documentation sur la Communaute; 48 IWM; 49 Assoc. des Francais Libres; 50 Doc. sur la Communaute; 50 Keystone; 51 Etablissement Cinematographique et Photographique des Armees; 51 US Archives; 52 Keystone; 52 Pictorial Press; 52 ECP-Armees; 53 Keystone; 54 Camera; 54 Assoc. des Francais Libres; 55 United Press International; 56-7 IWM; 58 Keystone; 61 Documentation Francaise; 62-3 IWM; 64 Popper; 65 Doc. Francaise; 66 Keystone; 67 Pictorial; 68-9 Keystone; 71 IWM; 72 Keystone; 74 US Archives; 74 Pictorial; 75 Viollet; 75 Popper; 76-7 US Archives; 79 Keystone; 80 Muracciole; 82 Keystone; 83 Comite de la 2 GM; 85 Assoc. des Francais Libres; 86-7 US Archives; 89 Camera/IWM; 90-1 Fox; 92 Keystone; 94 Doc. Francaise; 95 US Archives; 97 Doc. Francaise; 98-9 Psywar Society; 100-1 Keystone; 102-3 Doc. Francaise; 104-7 IWM; 108 Collin Belemont; 109 US Archives; 110 IWM; 112 Keystone; 112 Doc. Francaise; 114-6 OFIC, Paris; 116-9 Keystone; 121 ECP-Armees; 122-3 Belemont 124 US Army; 126-7 Keystone; 128 Camera/IWM; 129-30 IWM; 131 Camera; 132-3 US Archives; 134-5 IWM; 136 Camera/IWM; 138-9 Belemont; 140-1 ECP-Armees; 142-3 Keystone; 145-7 US Archives; 148-51 ECP-Armees; 152 Psywar; 154-5 Viollet; 157 Camera/IWM; 159 Fox; Front cover: US Army; Back cover: IWM

Copyright © 1972 Ballantine Books Inc.

First Printing: January 1972
Printed in United States of America

Ballantine Books Inc.
101 Fifth Avenue New York NY 10003

An Intext Publisher

Contents

9   Access to the truth

25   The turning point

35   The call of 18th June

47   Drama at Dakar

59   Conflict with the Allies

73   'Between East and West'

81   North Africa

93   The Maquis

111 The future in the balance

125 Victory

137 The tedious peace

Free French hero
Introduction by S.L. Mayer

Since 1789 France has tended to alternate between her liberal, revolutionary and democratic tradition and the authoritarian tendency which was her inheritance from the Bourbons and Louis XIV. From the bourgeois revolution of Siéyès and Lafayette came the proletarian Terror of Robespierre; from the democratic decadence of the Directory came Napoleon. Ever since the great revolutionary upheavals of the late Eighteenth Century France has vacillated between these divergent poles. Quite often long periods of quasi-democratic government have been followed by coup d'états and authoritarian rule in the name of the nation. Then, within a generation, fervor for the man on horseback waned and another coup, or perhaps a war, replaced the once-acclaimed leader. Take Napoleon III for example, the nephew of Bonaparte. He came to power in the mid-nineteenth century after a sequence of revolutionary upheavals, brought a period of stability (and colonial war, not to mention the Crimea and the Italian campaign of 1859), but his popularity waned in the 1860s, and at a moment when the authoritarian nature of his régime was changing, he was captured in the turmoil of French defeat at the hands of Prussia, taken to Germany, and his government fell apart, being replaced by the Paris Commune, German occupation, and the Third Republic, in roughly that order. It is ironic that the French often feel that their great achievements have taken place under the direction of the occasional popular dictator. In fact, their longest period of governmental stability in modern times was during the Third Republic, which kept France together albeit with difficulty during the First World War, and which was tottering toward major social reform when the invasion of 1940 brought its almost seventy-year-long tenure to an abrupt end.

Charles de Gaulle was a minor military figure during the First World War, and he served bravely under

Marshal Pétain, the hero of Verdun. During the interwar period he cautioned the French that mobile warfare would be the pattern in the next war. He, almost alone among French military writers of the time, recognized that the Maginot Line, both in its construction and philosophy, was not suited to the purposes of the coming war, a fact which was brutally borne out in the blitzkrieg of 1940. The German army, however, learned the lessons which de Gaulle taught very well indeed, and the panzer divisions which swept through northern France in the spring campaign of 1940 confirmed the unheeded warnings of both Captain Basil Liddell Hart and temporary Brigadier-General de Gaulle. In the death-throes of the Third Republic, in the humiliation of total defeat and the surrender negotiations at Compiègne, the French once again turned towards authoritarianism to save what was left of independent France. The hero of the First World War, Pétain, was charged with picking up the pieces after the defeat in the Second. France was partitioned, and a quasi-independent régime was established at Vichy to administer southeastern France and the colonial empire overseas. De Gaulle's road to greatness thus begins in the depths of despair. An authoritarian by nature himself, admired by and even an admirer of Pétain, de Gaulle chose to go it alone. He fled to England, and broadcast to the French people that under his leadership France could and would continue the fight, through her colonies, with the help of her allies. For the first time in its turbulent history France had two authoritarian régimes to choose from – Pétain's Vichy and de Gaulle's Free French. Some, regrettably, chose even a third – the Third Reich.

De Gaulle's isolation, his apparently solitary fight to maintain a corner of Free France in her darkest hour, became an inspiration to many. His indomitable personality and his intransigence became a thorn in the side to many others, not all of whom were sympathetic with the Axis. Roosevelt once told a distinguished foreign minister of one of the governments-in-exile who visited him that he thought de Gaulle was mad. Churchill, in that often-quoted remark, called him the greatest cross he had to bear, in characteristic overstatement. But the liberation of Paris, due largely to the strength of his Anglo-Saxon allies, was a triumph which was his own; a personal victory in the face of overwhelming odds. Philippe Masson describes this lonely fight of Charles de Gaulle, tracing his struggle from the days of humiliation in 1940 to the hours of triumph in 1944-45. He also explains how the fight to retain his authoritarian control over a liberated France was lost at the end of the war, and why de Gaulle chose retirement, again in a kind of splendid isolation, rather than to preside over the Fourth Republic, which had many of the faults which helped to weaken the Third. De Gaulle's second period of isolation, from his retirement in 1946 to his coup and return to power in 1958, proved once more the dual nature of French democracy; tired once again of the multi-party and multi-governmental pattern of the Fourth Republic, France chose to give her authoritarian hero another chance. One thing was certain, however. Whichever side won the Second World War, either Pétain or de Gaulle would find himself in the dock facing the wrath of an angry nation. As it turned out, it was de Gaulle who had the unenviable duty of placing his old commander before the bar of vengeance. It was characteristic of the man to ask clemency for the hero of Verdun, rather than the death penalty, for a man who had, in his time, given so much for France, and who, in his way, had inspired many Frenchmen in much the same way as de Gaulle had done. It is doubtful, had the shoe been on the other foot, that de Gaulle would have received similar treatment from Pétain had Hitler, rather than the Allies, won the war.

Access to the truth

By June 1940 the French armies were in full flight and nothing remained to block the advance of the victorious Panzers. At Briare and at Tours the Anglo-French alliance crumbled under the shock of events and the clash of national egos. On 14th June the Germans entered Paris. On the 16th, the Prime Minister, Paul Reynaud, handed in his resignation, making way for a government headed by Marshal Pétain, and served by General Weygand whose first job was to ask the enemy their conditions for an armistice, even a peace treaty. But during the late afternoon of 18th June a French acting brigadier-general of forty-nine, ex-Under Secretary for Defence in Paul Reynaud's Government, entered the BBC studios in London. He sat down in front of a microphone, unfolded a piece of paper and in a sombre voice exhorted the French people to carry on the struggle. 'Moi, Général de Gaulle . . .'

To the great majority of French people, General de Gaulle was unknown. Born in 1890, at Lille, Charles de Gaulle's family was part of the old order of society, of the now dispossessed gentry. They were profoundly Catholic and mourned the passing of the monarchy. Twenty years after its birth, they still refused to accept the secular Republic which they believed was falsely egalitarian and cut off from the nation's traditions. For Charles, as for his three brothers and sister, the imprint of his closely-knit family remained profound and indelible. It was in the confines of this conservative milieu that he developed a strong sense of duty, an unswerving and passionate patriotism, and a taste for authority.

His father's role was decisive in shaping his career. A teacher and then a headmaster in private schools, he instilled in his children a love of the French language, of literature and history. He often told his pupils: 'People say that history repeats itself. They are wrong. It is true that the same causes always produce the same effects, but history never goes back over the same ground.' At the family table the arts and history formed the basis for conversation: Racine, Corneille and the gallery of heroes from French history – Du Guesclin, Joan of Arc, Louis XIV, Napoleon. Sunday meant a visit to a museum or a walk in the eastern suburbs of Paris where Charles's father was wounded in the siege of 1870.

Charles de Gaulle was a brilliant scholar and he had a prodigious memory. For a while he toyed with the

Henri de Gaulle, Charles de Gaulle's father. A headmaster and a patriot, he was profoundly Catholic and mourned the passing of the monarchy

idea of the Polytechnique but decided instead on a military career and the college of Saint-Cyr. He chose the infantry and not the cavalry 'because there the field of action is infinitely more vast'. He left Saint-Cyr in 1912, finishing thirteenth out of 212.

De Gaulle began his military career as a young officer in the 33rd Infantry Regiment at Arras. Like most of the officers of his generation, he had to wait with secret impatience for the final test ... and the terrible disillusionment it brought. First, there was the formidable power of automatic gunfire. He was wounded on 15th August 1914 at Dinant in Belgium and noted: 'The affected calm of the officers who get themselves killed, bayonets fixed by some obstinate sections, trumpets sounding the charge, supreme efforts by isolated heroes, all for nothing. In one moment you realize that all the courage in the world is as nothing against gunfire.'

Then there was the war of the trenches – waiting, anguish, fear, and futile attacks. 'The hour of the attack draws near. Nervous tension reaches a peak. Watches are constantly pulled out of pockets. The commanders can feel the eyes fixed on them. Forcing themselves to keep calm, they pace along the lines, point out the objective, give directions. The bonds of discipline tighten around each man ... The time has come. The officers make a sign. Behind them, automatically, with dry throats and throbbing temples, the men rise to attack.'

In 1915 de Gaulle was made a captain and wounded again in Champagne. In February 1916 he was at Verdun at Fort Douaumont where his company was decimated under a terrible bombardment. The young captain was wounded once more and taken prisoner.

De Gaulle was transferred to Germany and sent to several camps before ending up at Fort IX at Ingolstadt. After an abortive attempt to escape he buried his boredom in study. He gave several lectures to his comrades and became interested in the first tanks that appeared. He studied reports on military and civil power in Germany and later, in 1924, published a book on the subject *Discord in the Enemy Camp*.

When he was freed at the beginning of 1919 de Gaulle's career differed little from that of many of his comrades. As an instructor, he went with the French military mission to Poland. Then he returned to France and taught history at Saint-Cyr. From 1922 to 1924 he was at the Ecole de Guerre before entering Marshal Pétain's cabinet. After a command in the 19th Rifles at Trier, he spent a period in the Middle East, in Beirut, and then joined the Ministry of Defence where he remained from 1930 to 1937. In 1926 he was married to Yvonne Vendroux, a girl of good social standing whose family came from northern France. But before long tragedy struck the young household. The third child, Anne, was born in 1928. She was a mongol, who gave the de Gaulles twenty years of heartache and who died in 1948.

Let us pause a while and take our

The young officer cadet at Saint-Cyr military college. A brilliant scholar with a good memory, he graduated 13th out of 212 in 1912

Prisoner of war, 1917. Now a captain, he was wounded and captured on the Verdun front in February 1916 and remained in captivity for the duration

bearings. In 1930, at the age of forty, de Gaulle had just been promoted to lieutenant-colonel. In spite of the protection he was given by Pétain, who continued to influence him and who was godfather to his son, de Gaulle's future remained uncertain. He had a reputation in the army for eccentricity, nonconformism, and unconventional ideas. His physical characteristics alone worked against him. He was immensely tall – at Saint-Cyr they called him 'yardstick' – often ill at ease, clumsy and slow. He was a rotten horseman. His face was long and heavy, with small fleshy lips and not much chin. There was something effete about his appearance but his eyes always had an exceptional sparkle. His voice was colourless, some described it as 'nocturnal'.

Nevertheless, the young colonel was distinguished by his ardour for work, the loftiness of his ideas, his wide cultural knowledge, his prodigious memory and a remarkable ability to synthesize the elements of a problem and find its solution. As a history teacher at Saint-Cyr he ruled his pupils with a rod of iron. Like many of his comrades de Gaulle was driven by the urge to write. *The Sword's Edge* and *The Army of the Future*, both written before *France and her Army*, were remarkable for the erudition and quality of their style. His sentences were classically inspired, studded with quotations and, although sometimes heavy, were touched with a spark of brilliance.

His superiors and his equals alike recognised his genius and mockingly termed him 'the future generalissimo'. De Gaulle was short-tempered, easily provoked, and quick to take offence. It is true that he deigned to frequent certain salons and, on occasions, even showed himself to be a highly gifted conversationalist much appreciated by the ladies; but for the most part he was arrogant and aloof. De Gaulle never indulged himself, and it seemed that he was fated to be a lonely man. He had hardly any friends. He was

Pétain, the Grand Old Man of the French army. He was the young de Gaulle's protector, and godfather to his son

already a man set apart, cloaked in a lofty solitude, convinced of his own superiority, and consumed with veiled ambition. When he was a prisoner of war his comrades nicknamed him 'The Commander-in-Chief' and among the reports on him at the Ecole de Guerre one noted that he 'unfortunately spoils undeniable qualities by excessive self-confidence, unwillingness to listen to other people's opinions and behaviour like a king in exile . . .'

Throughout his career at the distinguished college his 'complacency' and 'refusal to tolerate criticism' was a source of irritation to his teachers. Moreover, he appeared to disregard the practical aspect of problems and refused to involve himself in details. This had its effect on his grading when he left. He came in the 'second third' category, with the mention 'Good'. De Gaulle did not hide his bitterness and rage: 'Those bastards at the Ecole de Guerre! . . . I shan't stay in that filthy hole unless they make me Commanding Officer of the college. It'll all change, you'll see! . . .' Pétain was infuriated by this affront to his protégé, and in 1927 de Gaulle took his revenge on the college. In the Marshal's presence, he delivered a series of lectures to the assembled teachers and students of the college entitled *War and Leadership, Character, and Prestige*. The lectures had a stupendous effect. De Gaulle confronted his audience in full dress, with his sword and white gloves laid out in front of him; he spoke without notes and embellished his lectures with literary and philosophic allusions. But this performance served only to increase his isolation and aroused much bitterness and jealousy.

De Gaulle once wrote of Pétain that his character contained 'a large admixture of egoism, pride, toughness and guile' and exactly the same could be said of de Gaulle himself. It is, perhaps, not unreasonable to suggest that when he wrote those words about Pétain, he was transposing his own character onto that of his hero. He

Above: British troops enter a fort on the Maginot Line, the concrete realisation of the French army's tactic of the supposedly 'inviolable' defensive front which de Gaulle criticised so bitterly in the 1930s. *Below:* French troops on manoeuvres near the German frontier, 1938

instinctively identified himself with the line of commanders who were out of step with the rest, those who knew how to dominate and how to disobey.

'I do not know of any officer who was more hated,' said one general of de Gaulle. This thinly disguised hostility arose largely because of de Gaulle's criticism of the official teaching and the narrow frame of mind which prevailed in the army. To a great extent, he was already regarded as a rebel. One has only to recall the general state of the French military system in the 1930s to understand this attitude. At that time the army was resting on the laurels it had won in the First World War, falling prey to a creeping paralysis and stagnation. Certain that they possessed the key to victory, the distinguished generals of 1918 were ageing at their posts and endeavouring to make rules of the lessons they had learned during the war. Sheltered by the rampart of the Maginot Line, designed to allow time for mobilization and to avoid all risks of surprise, when the army envisaged war it envisaged an 'organized' and methodical battle, safe from the vagaries of chance and surprise. The generals busied themselves with the 'inviolable' defensive fronts. They looked no further than the 'sections of terrain', the slow attack preceded by intense artillery bombardment, the infantry acting in strict liaison with the tanks. There was no question of breakthrough, only 'continuous lines rolling forward like a procession'.

Strategy and history were left aside. The preoccupations of the generals remained purely tactical. In the words of General Beaufre, they envisaged a 'war of contractors . . . where one parcels out the land in man-miles, artillery-miles and shell-miles.' Such formal tactics ruled out mobility and chance, stifled the imagination and the offensive spirit and made nonsense of a diplomacy which entailed serious obligations to certain Eastern European countries.

Since 1918, the French army had not only come to a standstill, it had regressed. Under these circumstances it was hardly surprising that many of the younger officers were worried about the army's teaching, that they felt it was severely lacking in inspiration and drive. But in de Gaulle, concern became dispute. Disregarding military hierarchy, he condemned the prevailing order and did not hesitate to make the quarrel public.

It was in 1934 that a turning point came. De Gaulle had no illusions about the conventional wisdom and he was determined to be its leading critic. His two major works appeared in close succession. *The Sword's Edge* and *The Army of the Future*. They claimed to present a new solution to the French military problem; the young colonel's thought was put forward as an organic whole, which could be summarized in three words: contingency, character and machine.

De Gaulle's first intention was to rehabilitate some of the essential principles of the military art. He was much influenced by Bergson, and believed in the virtues of intuition and instinct. He roundly condemned the official dogmatism. 'War', he said, 'is essentially bound up with contingency. The outcome pursued in war is relative to the enemy, who is pre-eminently changeable: he can present himself in a multitude of ways; he has resources at his command whose exact strength one does not know and he can reach his objectives by many different routes. This contingency which is an essential characteristic of war is at once its drawback and its greatness.' This statement implies a veto on *a priori* reasoning and a condemnation without appeal of 'the spirit of system building'.

Nevertheless, the very complexity of the act of war demands an antidote to the moral enfeeblement of the army and a rehabilitation of character and the will. It was during the 1927 lectures sponsored by Pétain that

Heinz Guderian, Germany's armoured warfare theoretician. When de Gaulle's writings on the role of tanks were translated into German Guderian noted their similarity to his own

de Gaulle presented his ideas on the 'charisma of the leader', and these were later repeated almost verbatim in *The Sword's Edge*. 'Our time', he stated, 'is not propitious for training and selecting military leaders. The trials we have recently undergone have caused our wills to weaken and our characters to sag. A moral lassitude erodes the belief in order which is necessary for war, and attacks even the most resolute of vocations . . .'

He goes on to describe the traits of the 'man of character' who 'embraces action with the pride of the owner, for he is caught up with it, and it is his; he rejoices in success provided he has deserved it and even though he may gain nothing from it; he sustains reverses of fortune, not without a certain bitter satisfaction.' At critical times it is men of this stamp, men who exude a natural 'air of authority', to whom the army must turn. 'A sort of ground swell thrusts to the forefront the man of character. His advice is taken, his talents praised, his ability trusted. The difficult task, the principal effort, the decisive mission – all these are naturally his.'

But the predestined man, or simply the leader, must have at his right hand the instrument which suits his need for action, which is capable of moving with the rhythm of a changing reality, in tune with the geographic and diplomatic needs of France. *The Army of the Future* seeks to fulfil these requirements and forms the last section of de Gaulle's thought: after contingency and character, now the machine. This work, by far the most famous, is a broadsheet for the internal combustion engine, the armoured machine.

De Gaulle stated that six armoured divisions with 4,000 tanks manned by regular soldiers, would constitute a striking force worthy of France's temperament and political aspirations, 'an awesome system of mechanical skill, gunfire, shock, speed and camouflage'. 'The troops of today,' he wrote, 'are the machines, coupled with teams trained to serve them.' This battle corps would make it possible to offset the dissolute tendencies of the existing army which 'screens itself with facades'. 'A liking for what is clean, clipped, compact, this is the driving force behind our highly trained and vigorous youth. But how can it subsist in an army which is perpetually condemned to "getting by"?' De Gaulle believed that the new army should bring the return of the war of movement, of breakthrough, of the chase. It would be an integral part of the 'contingency' which is inherent in all true military action. It would permit the army to 'spring surprise, ancient queen of the art'.

Scarcely had the book appeared than it gave rise to bitter polemics. But it could not have been called a prophetic work, ahead of its time. De Gaulle himself was aware that his ideas were not revolutionary. He was merely restating the problem. In Great Britain, General Fuller and Sir Basil Liddell Hart had already pin-

A Renault R-35 in manoeuvres

French light tanks – the neglected arm

pointed the merits of tanks, showing that they combined the advantages of both artillery and cavalry. The British army had already carried out interesting experiments on Salisbury Plain. In Germany, Captain Heinz Guderian had arrived at similar conclusions. He had experimented with tanks at Cambrai and with the formidable combination of tanks and an air division in 1918. He had also been influenced by the Austrian General, von Eimannsberger, who was about to publish *Tank Warfare*. Nevertheless, de Gaulle's work was translated into German. Guderian found in it only a confirmation of his own ideas and it is interesting to note that the German military attachés in France never mentioned the theories contained in *The Army of the Future* in their dispatches.

In France itself, more than ten years had elapsed since Colonel Estienne announced the advent of modern warfare: 'Think, Gentlemen,' he had said, 'of the formidable advantages, both strategic and tactical, which would accrue to the heaviest armies of the past few years: 100,000 men capable of covering fifty miles in a single night . . . Imagine breakthrough tanks of fifty to one hundred tons . . . crushing all obstacles, disembowelling houses. The armoured infantry and the accompanying artillery. Soon the first enemy lines are crushed and the light tanks rush forward, as the cavalry once did, to seal the victory.' And in 1928 Colonel Doumenc had set in motion a project for an armoured division, forerunner of the Panzers.

Above all, de Gaulle's book was a manifesto, a firebrand hurled at the citadels of conformism, at the General Staff and its offspring, the Ecole de Guerre. Only in this sense can one term it a revolutionary book and it is this which explains the violence and above all the nature of the criticism which greeted it.

De Gaulle's ideas had come up against a brick wall of principle. With the star of totalitarian régimes in the ascendant, France – shattered by the First World War divided both politically and socially, riddled with doubt – refused or simply felt unable to adopt a breakthrough army, for this presupposed will, energy, decision it no longer had. The French military

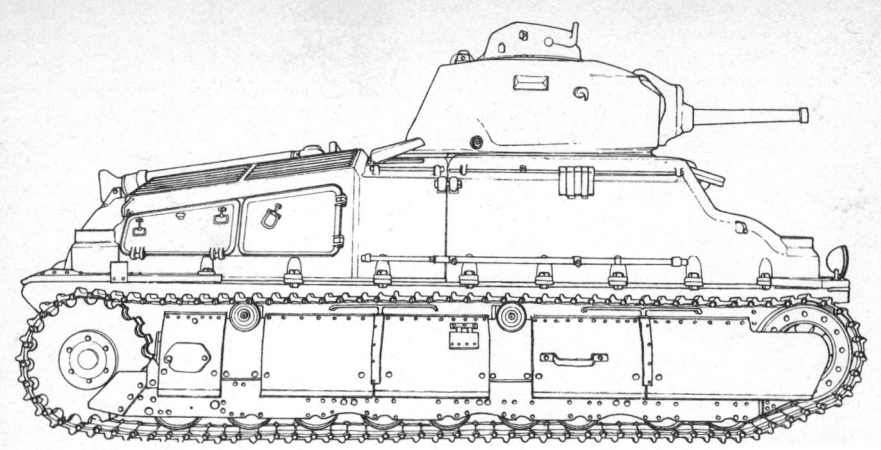

The SOMUA S35, the main equipment of French medium tank units in 1940, was one of the best tanks of its day. About 500 had been produced up to the time of the German invasion. *Weight:* 19.5 tons. *Crew:* 3. *Armament:* one 47mm gun with 118 rounds and one 7.5mm Reibel machine gun with 3,000 rounds. *Armour:* 40mm *Power:* SOMUA V-8, 190hp. *Speed:* 29 mph on roads, 11 mph cross country. *Trench crossing:* 7 feet. *Step:* 2 feet 6 inches. *Radius of action:* 143 miles. *Length:* 17 feet 6 inches. *Height:* 8 feet 7½ inches. *Width:* 6 feet 11 inches

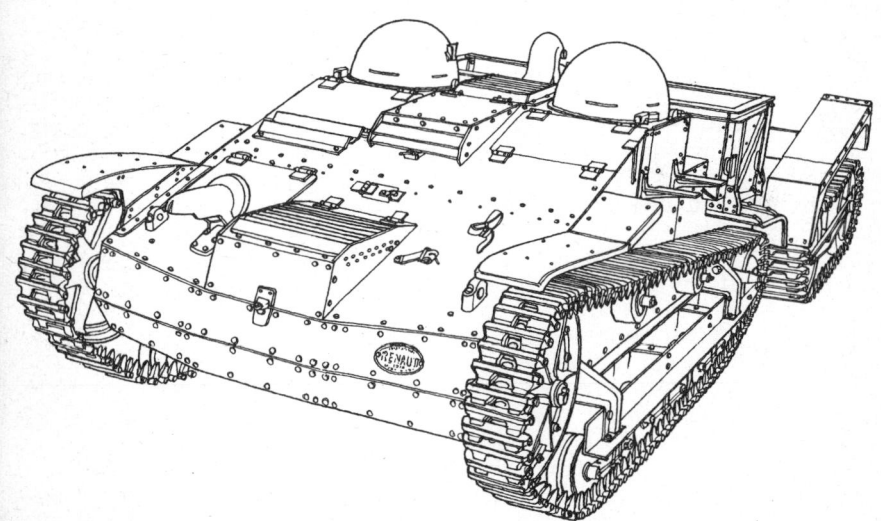

The French Renault UE Chenillette Model 1931 tractor/carrier. The design of this vehicle was clearly a development and improvement of the basic pattern evolved in the FT series of the First World War, the main feature of which was the much larger radius of the return rollers at the front of the track than the drive wheels at the rear. *Weight:* 2.5 metric tons unladen, 2.8 laden. *Crew:* 2. *Armament:* One 7.5mm machine gun. *Armour:* 4mm minimum, 7mm maximum (too lightly armoured for even early Second World War conditions). *Engine:* 4-cylinder Renault. *Speed:* 19mph. *Range:* 110 miles. *Length:* 8.9 feet. *Width:* 5.9 feet. *Height:* 5.6 feet

General Gamelin, French C-in-C. 'I do not believe in Colonel de Gaulle's theories. As for the air force . . . it will be a flash in the pan'

doctrine, based upon the defensive, the continuous front, the supporting tank, only reflected a state of mind. France would defend herself if she was attacked but she refused to carry war beyond her frontiers. With the exception of de Gaulle, no one underlined the fact that this attitude was incompatible with her obligations towards Czechoslovakia and Poland. But France no longer wished to draw her sword; at most she would brandish a shield.

The fiercest opposition to de Gaulle came from military circles. A three-star general declared in the *Mercure de France:* 'A pacifist and defensive France can only be opposed to motorization.' Weygand grated: 'We will not have two armies at any price . . . we have all we need, nothing needs forming'. The most interesting criticisms are perhaps Pétain's. In the preface to General Chevineau's book, *Is Invasion Still Possible?* he expressed his belief that the tank would be crushed just like the infantry in 1914, not by machine guns but by anti-tank guns, mines and obstacles of every sort. In a sense the old Marshal seems to have foreseen the state of armoured warfare in 1944-45 when the tank ceased to rule the battlefield. In his turn, the Minister of War, General Maurin, declared: 'Do they think we are fool enough to go beyond this barrier [the Maginot Line] to God knows what sort of adventure?'

For his part the Commander-in-Chief, General Gamelin, declared to a Member of Parliament: 'I do not believe in Colonel de Gaulle's theories. They are unsound and unrealistic. Tanks are necessary, it is true. But to think that with tanks you can crush the whole organization of the enemy, is just not serious . . . The tank is not endowed with self-sufficiency. It has to go through, but it has to come back for more fuel and ammunition. As for the air force . . . it will be a flash in the pan.'

The army, then, condemned his ideas as metaphysical and unworkable. General Maurin decided to dismiss the colonel from the Secretariat of the Ministry of Defence and to send him to the 507th Tank Regiment stationed at Metz. 'You have caused us enough trouble with the tank on paper, now let's see what you can make of the real thing!' he told de Gaulle. On arrival, de Gaulle plunged into furious activity to the horror of Supplies who complained about the 'abnormal' wear on tracks and engines. General Giraud, the commanding officer, pointed a menacing finger at him: 'As long as I am in command here, you and your theories, my little Gaulle . . .'

In civilian and parliamentary circles, *The Army of the Future* was criticized in different ways. Its title, purposely provocative and controversial, caused a stir on the Left. It seemed to ridicule the sacrosanct principles of the national army and had an odour of 'pronunciamento' about it. As for the Socialists and Radicals, they thought they heard the menacing footsteps of the Prætorian Guard. Yet Leon Blum was, in his heart of hearts, seduced by the theories of 'this man cast in a single mould'. Several newspapers, like *l'Echo de*

The Char 1B- and B-1bis formed the basis of the equipment used by the French armoured divisions in 1940. About 500 of the latter model, which differed from the early only in modifications to ease production, were available at the time of the German invasion. *Weight:* 31 tons. *Crew:* 4. *Armament:* one 75mm gun in hull with 77 rounds (but no traverse), one 47mm gun in turret with 50 rounds (360° traverse) and two 7.5mm Reibel machine guns. *Armour:* 20mm minimum, 60mm maximum. *Power:* Renault water-cooled inline 307hp. *Speed:* 18 mph. *Trench crossing:* 9 feet. *Step:* 3 feet 10 inches. *Radius of action:* 130 miles. *Length:* 20 feet 11 inches. *Height:* 9 feet 2 inches. *Width:* 8 feet 2 inches

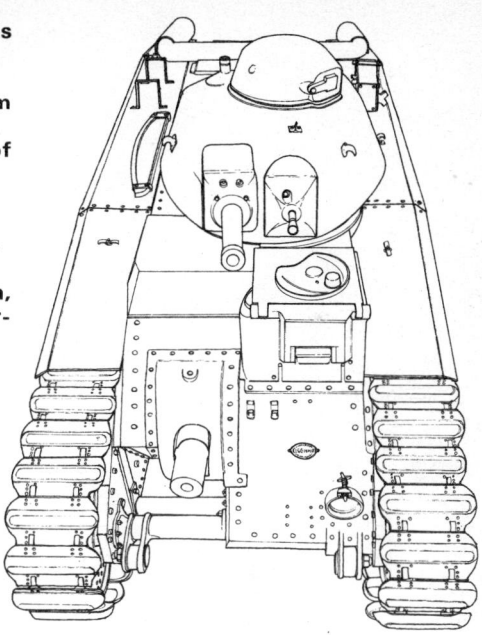

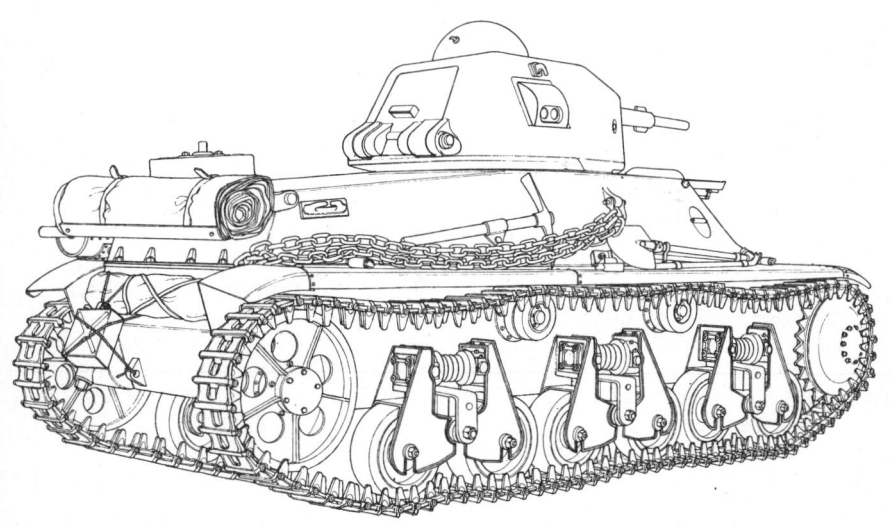

The French Char H 39/40. The Hotchkiss H 39/40 was a development of the H 35, and was used by the French armoured cavalry divisions in 1940. *Weight:* 12 tons. *Crew:* 2. *Armament:* One 37mm gun and one machine gun. *Speed:* 25mph. *Radius of action:* 120 miles. *Engine:* Hotchkiss 6-cylinder, 120hp. *Armour:* 20mm minimum, 40mm maximum. *Length:* 13 feet 10 inches. *Width:* 6 feet 5 inches. *Height:* 7 feet 1 inch

Paul Reynaud. His Bill for the creation of 'a mechanised army of quality' was defeated early in 1935

Paris, l'*Epoque*, le *Temps* or le *Journal des Débats* mounted a press campaign in support of de Gaulle's theories. *L'Action Française*, under the byline of its defence correspondent, showed a keen interest in a motorized army. Several deputies from the Right and Centre lent their support to de Gaulle's ideas and on 15th March 1935, Paul Reynaud presented a bill to the Chamber concerning the creation of a 'mechanized army of quality', comprising seven divisions which should be completely established 'by 15th April 1940 at the very latest . . . ' The Bill was defeated.

Thus, at the time when Hitler was beginning to upset European peace, de Gaulle cut a solitary figure. He was in a state of moral revolt against the army, that great sick corpse with its atrophied imagination which was condemning his ideas. The final break with Pétain dates from this time, although his protection had seen de Gaulle through some sticky times. Between 1925 and 1927 he had acted as ghost-writer to the Marshal who loathed writing but set himself up as an elegant stylist. The old leader contented himself with using a blue pencil on texts written by members of his 'house' and giving them his personal stamp. But for de Gaulle by 1938 Pétain was nothing more than a 'doddering old man', 'dead since 1925', prisoner of a 'senile ambition', and a 'monster of pride and hard-heartedness'.

From now on, in increasing isolation, de Gaulle gave full rein to his resentment and his anxiety. He was one of the few senior officers who had their eyes open and who foresaw the extent of the catastrophe facing Europe. In 1936, at the time of the remilitarization of the Rhineland, he declared: 'We should have taken them by surprise, with brutality and with speed . . . It is a disaster, no doubt irreparable . . . If we had had my professional army and my tanks . . . we should have advanced and the Germans retreated . . . Peace would have been assured.' For the time being de Gaulle felt more and more attracted towards politics. He haunted the antechambers of various members of parliament – although his visits were eclectic: Leftists like Philippe Serre,

Léo Lagrange, Marcel Déat, and a Right-wing deputy, Paul Reynaud. But even there, disillusion awaited him. After an interview with Léon Blum, he was led to the conclusion that the 'system' was impotent.

Later, he said of this period: 'Before the war I thought in the same way as every officer of my generation: Parliament, crises, the instability of power, the parties . . . ' Temperament and training put his sympathies clearly on the side of an authoritarian régime. It is true he kept well away from *L'Action Française* but he had dedicated his first book, *Discord in the Enemy Camp*, to Maurras and he gradually drew closer to the Christian Democrats, convinced of the importance of social questions.

Thus, on the eve of war, he was the one man in France who possessed a rare military and strategic lucidity, but also a man 'cast in a single mould', broken loose from an army which repudiated him. This ostracism served only to strengthen his natural tendencies: isolation, arrogance, contempt, and the terrible pride of the man who has an inner conviction that he has special access to the truth.

A page had been turned. De Gaulle no longer expected anything from the army. His ambition was 'cosmic' and, like a hero of Stendhal, de Gaulle thought in his most secret meditations that *le Rouge*, the profession of arms, would enable him to attain the greatest heights. From childhood he had been convinced that one day he would be called upon to render France 'a signal service'. To a friend who once said to him, 'I have a curious feeling that you are bound for a very great destiny', he contented himself with replying: 'Yes . . ., so have I.'

In *The Edge of the Sword* politics and soldiery did not cease to haunt him. His preoccupations turned towards Alexander the Great, Frederick II, Napoleon, men who knew how to reconcile the military art with the art of government. He believed that 'everything which the masses formerly

Léon Blum, leader of France's Popular Front government. He was seduced by de Gaulle's theories, but made it clear that they could never be adopted by the army command

accorded to office and birth, they now reserve for men who have known how to assert themselves. What lawful prince was ever obeyed like a dictator who has nothing behind him except his own daring? The leader who commands, on whatever rung of the ladder, must rely for his following, less on his superior position than his personal qualities. One should not confuse power with its attributes.'

To be sure, de Gaulle did not feel any vocation for the part of colonel in a *pronunciamento*. The military leader, he reiterated, should not operate outside the framework of the state, but should wait until circumstances, an *event*, thrusts him to the forefront. Then should he identify himself with the state, 'take over' the Fatherland. There can be no doubt that de Gaulle felt he belonged to the legion of predestined leaders, awaiting the 'Call'. It was not without a secret impatience that he awaited the new test: 'at the first flash of swords, our system of values will be overthrown.'

The turning point

The crisis came on 3rd September 1939. De Gaulle found himself in the same position as Pétain twenty-five years before him: the same rank, his promotion compromised, a too-well established reputation for nonconformism. But he felt a secret satisfaction. In the long run, would not the war 'lavish bitter caresses' upon him and allow him to answer the insistent call of destiny? In the meantime he had the satisfaction of knowing he had seen the problems clearly. In 1914 his doctrine had been 'bullets kill', in 1939 that the tank was the instrument of breakthrough. No one would deny he had been right on the first count, and now the Polish campaign brought startling confirmation on the second. In less than three weeks, mechanical power, together with imagination and daring, broke the resistance of the valiant Polish army. And Gamelin's estimate for Poland's stand had been six months.

But at the head of the 507th Tank Regiment in Alsace, de Gaulle was growing pessimistic. He was one of the few French military leaders to understand the full significance of

De Gaulle, now commander of 4th Armoured Division, with Daladier, French War Minister

the tactical combination of tank and aircraft. Greeting a group of British MPs he said: 'Gentlemen, this war is lost . . . We must therefore prepare ourselves for another which we shall win, with the machine.' He told Léon Blum of his anguish: 'I am playing my part in a hideous delusion . . . The few dozen light tanks that I command are but a drop in the ocean. I fear that the lesson we have learned from Poland, although so clear, has been deliberately ignored. They will not admit that what succeeded there should be practised here . . . If we do not act in time, we shall be miserably defeated in this war . . . '

It was thus that he decided to act. He took what for an officer was a grave step. On 24th January he sent eighty civilian and military personalities a memorandum entitled *The advent of mechanized power*. This manifesto was a condensed version of the ideas contained in *The Army of the Future*, revised in the light of the invasion of Poland. First it condemned the 'Phoney War': 'in the present conflict, to be passive is to admit defeat. The French people must at no cost labour under the illusion that the present military immobility would be consistent with the nature of the present war. The opposite is true.

Blitzkrieg – German armoured might invades Poland

The internal combustion engine has given to modern methods of destruction a power, a speed and a range of action such that the present conflict will sooner or later be marked by movement, surprise, invasion and pursuit, the volume and speed of which will infinitely exceed that of the most astounding events of the past...'

He also had a premonition of the course the war would take. 'Let us not be mistaken! The war which has begun could well be the most far-reaching, the most complex and the most violent of all conflicts which have ravaged the earth. The political, social and moral crisis which has precipitated it is of such magnitude that it will end fatally with the complete disruption of peoples and states...'

De Gaulle called for the immediate establishment of independent armoured divisions, supported by a strong arm of fighter aircraft. There was little response to this call, and Reynaud, who had become Prime Minister on 21st May, did not succeed in appointing de Gaulle as secretary to the Comité de Guerre because of the opposition of the War Minister, Daladier. But Gamelin decided to give the young leader the command of the 4th Armoured Division which was then being trained and would be ready for active service on about 15th May.

It had been in 1938, after many hesitations, that Gamelin had decided to create armoured divisions. In fact, these were only a caricature of the Panzer divisions or of the formations advocated by Doumenc and de Gaulle. They were merely a conglomeration of tank battalions endowed with a few accompanying infantry elements, not a true independent unit with armour, cross-country vehicles, anti-aircraft anti-tank artillery and logistical support. In reality, the French armoured divisions were intended merely for counterattack within the framework of a defensive strategy.

On 10th May Germany turned the *Blitzkrieg* westwards. On the 13th and 14th the front was broken at the Meuse. On the 15th the breakthrough was completed by Guderian's armoured crops which, when it arrived at Montcornet, found the way clear right through to the coast. The same day General Doumenc invited de Gaulle to counterattack northwards near Laôn, in an attempt to slow the advance of the Panzers.

On the 17th the 4th Armoured Division went into action. After advancing for nearly twenty miles they were forced to withdraw to the positions from which they had started out, harassed by Stukas and elements of the enemy's light armoured forces. On the 19th, a new attempt was made on the Serre. Guderian experienced 'several hours of uncertainty' and the French tanks came to within a mile of his advanced command post. In fact, the counterattack failed to hinder the inexorable progress of the German armour, which reached the sea the following day. Finally, on 28th May, the 4th Armoured Division attempted to demolish the German bridgehead across the Somme at Abbeville – an indispensable prelude to the relief of the

May 1940. The Blitzkrieg turns against France

encircled armies of the north – and almost succeeded. 400 German prisoners fell into French hands, but the armoured strike came to grief on the German Ju88s. Despite an 'atmosphere of victory' the division had yet again to be satisfied with a half-success.

The three body blows dealt by de Gaulle's 4th Armoured Division were the subject of much comment, not all of which was favourable. General Perré, a specialist in armoured forces and leader of the 2nd Armoured Division, conceded that de Gaulle's method of battle was 'classic' and that he was no longer to be regarded as a 'novice theorist'. But compared with the German line of attack, his was too wide and did not allow for sufficient concentration of resources. These criticisms appear to be valid. However, it must be borne in mind that the 4th Armoured Division had only just been formed, that it was still 'being broken in' and was seriously lacking in resources. Although there was a large number of tanks which were well armed and solidly protected, they were, after all, only machines for accompanying the infantry, slow and with a limited range of action. The crews had only just completed their training. The infantry was limited to a few companies travelling in requisitioned buses, and the 4th Armoured Division lacked both anti-aircraft defence and logistical support. The signals were glaringly inadequate and the division had to fall back on motorcycle dispatch-riders for communications. Nevertheless, from these half-successes, history has retained one important element: of all the generals involved in the tragic fall of France, de Gaulle was one of the few who did not retreat and who managed to impose his will on the enemy.

De Gaulle relinquished his command of the 4th Armoured Division after the Abbeville episode. On 5th June, he was made Under-Secretary of State for Defence by Paul Reynaud. It was an entry into politics by the side-door, but in the most dramatic circumstances imaginable. From 5th June there were no more illusions about the outcome of the Battle of France. After the tragedies at Lille and Dunkirk, the French army, reduced to some fifty divisions, could hope for no more on the Somme and the Aisne than to forestall the final reckoning and to save its honour. In the course of one of the most tragic weeks in the history of France, de Gaulle concentrated his every effort on securing the triumph of his policy: complete refusal to capitulate and continuation of the struggle from the coasts of Great Britain and North Africa, with the support of the fleet.

To this end, he mounted a campaign on several fronts. Firstly, he endeavoured to strengthen the wavering resolve of Paul Reynaud, who was being pressurized by Marshal Pétain and General Weygand, both converts to the idea of an armistice. On 12th June Paul Reynaud accepted the idea of transferring the government to Algiers. But this was labour lost. From the 14th, the Premier, now in Bordeaux, had virtually resigned.

De Gaulle also pestered Weygand, trying to convince him of the merits of his scheme. He believed that while there was still time, the General Headquarters should muster thousands of tanks and armoured cars from the different armies among which they were dispersed. They should then counterattack, disrupt the Germans' rear, and cut off their lines of communication. He believed that they should prepare the 500,000 men cramming the barracks for evacuation to North Africa, and send troops from Narvik and elsewhere, at the same time diverting to Casablanca the transport ships carrying American goods. He also tried to persuade them to keep hold of the navies, both merchant and marine, and the air force person-

Dunkirk. British and French prisoners march into captivity. France is shortly to capitulate

nel; to conceive a grand strategy and wrench themselves free from thinking in terms of the narrow confines of the capital.

Again he was brushed off. It seems that the Generalissimo merely laughed in the face of the Under Secretary for War. On the strength of General Darlan's opinion, Weygand would not hear of a massive withdrawal to North Africa. The Luftwaffe would stand in the way and the shipping would not be available. 'The Empire? Childish nonsense!' As for the rest of the world,' he said, 'when I have been beaten here, not a week will pass before Great Britain enters into negotiations with the Reich.'

De Gaulle's next card was the famous Brittany redoubt, although in his memoirs he did not admit to it. Certainly, he had never indulged in the hope of a prolonged resistance along a line from Saint Mâlo to Nantes. But his activities on 9th, 12th, and 15th June at Rennes and at Brest prove that his true aim in broaching the 'chimera' of the redoubt was to entice the government to Brittany and force it to depart for Africa from the port of Quimper. But there again, the scheme was short lived.

Finally, the Under-Secretary of State turned towards Great Britain. On 9th June he had his first meeting with Churchill. He then went to London to ask for the massive intervention of the RAF in the final battle. He met with a refusal. But the two men sized one another up and found mutual respect. On the 12th, at Briare, it was obvious that they were in sympathy with one another. But the warm eloquence of the British Prime Minister could not sway the majority of the French people who had rallied to the armistice. Nevertheless, in London on the 16th, de Gaulle accepted the strange proposition of an Anglo-French union, drawn up by

The Germans meet resistance on the Aisne, but this merely forestalls the final reckoning

carry on the struggle, and to refuse to capitulate. According to him, this major decision was taken as early as 16th May, as he watched the fleeing remnants of the Second Army at Montcornet. Perhaps. In any case, as far as the army was concerned, de Gaulle had been in a state of moral revolt ever since he left the Ecole de Guerre. For many years he had been preparing himself intellectually to seize his chance and assume responsibility for the nation, should the state collapse. The crisis came in the most tragic way possible, but not all the reasons for his decision were intimately connected with France's tragedy. There were others, more practical and immediate. Without taking too literal a view of Spear's account, of which there is not one

Admiral Darlan advised Weygand against de Gaulle's plan for a massive withdrawal to French North Africa

General Weygand. He and Pétain were the chief advocates of an Armistice

Jean Monnet and the French ambassador, Corbin. Churchill gave his approval, but with some hesitation. It was, in fact, a final scheme intended to strengthen the position of Paul Reynaud and to convince Pétain and Weygand of Britain's determination to fight. But the reception it received at Bordeaux was cool. Even the opponents of an armistice were reluctant to see France reduced to the level of a dominion.

When de Gaulle arrived at Bordeaux on the evening of 16th June, on his return from London, he found the country in chaos. Reynaud had just resigned. There was no government and the State had collapsed. De Gaulle was no longer Under-Secretary of State but only an acting brigadier general. That very evening he made his decision – to return to London, to

word in the famous memoirs, de Gaulle could, in fact, have been in danger of arrest. He might well have found himself in the company of Mandel and General Buhrer who Pétain had just imprisoned. And even if things did not actually come to such a pass, he could expect no more from the Marshal and Weygand. These two men, about to form a new government, had been the two great cornerstones of the French army between the wars. Furthermore there was the 'force of destiny' pressing him forward. Later, he was to say 'People often think that all this was prepared, premeditated. I do not think so. I felt myself guided by a hand stronger than mine. I was seized by an idea. I became the instrument of a will which was beyond my understanding.

'In the first days of the Battle of France, before I was called to the government, I could see only one way out for myself, poor colonel that I was: to die on the battlefield at the head of my regiment.

'In short, what I did was in some way imposed on me.'

On 17th June, armed with a viaticum of 100,000 francs taken out of secret funds, de Gaulle left Bordeaux for England. It was a departure 'without romanticism' according to the General. De Gaulle arrived in London in the afternoon of the 17th just when Marshal Pétain's radio broadcast was finishing: '. . . I offer France the gift of my person to assuage her ills. It is with a heavy heart that I tell you today that we must give up the struggle.' Churchill received the ex-Under-Secretary of State immediately and he believed there to be advantages in his action. He felt it might be a sign of the imminent arrival in London of a cohort of highly representative political personalities: Mandel, Reynaud . . . The British Prime Minister immediately placed at the General's disposal the radio, that unrivalled technical resource without which this incredible story would never have taken place.

Churchill. He welcomed de Gaulle to London and assured him of Britain's determination to fight on

The Call of 18th June

The next day, late in the afternoon, General de Gaulle entered the studios of the BBC and in front of the microphone launched the famous Appeal which was, in his own words, 'to change the face of the earth' – or at least to play a determining role in French history: 'The leaders who have been, for many years, at the head of the French armies have formed a government. This government, alleging the defeat of our armies, has entered into dealings with the enemy to end the fighting . . . But has the last word been said? Should hope die? Is the defeat total? No . . . France is not alone! She is not alone! She is not alone! This war is not limited to the territory of our unhappy country. This war is a world war . . . Struck down today by mechanized force, we shall conquer another day with superior mechanized force. I, General de Gaulle at present in London, call on the French officers and soldiers who find themselves on British territory . . . the engineers and the skilled workers of the armament industries . . . to join me. Whatever happens, the

De Gaulle makes his epic appeal for French patriots to join him in Britain, the day after Pétain had broadcast France's capitulation

flame of French resistance must not and shall not die . . . Tomorrow, as today, I shall speak on the radio from London.'

This message, beamed across the waves, was an epic event. First of all it was an act of faith. De Gaulle was confident of Great Britain's capacity for resistance. In the context of a world war, the defeat of France, or rather of her armies, was only the first act, albeit infinitely dramatic and distressing. 'France has lost a battle, she has not lost the war,' he wrote two days later. Secondly, the call of 18th June was a tremendous individual challenge. At last, the occasion for which he had been waiting since childhood, of rendering France 'a signal service', presented itself. The 'Moi, Général de Gaulle' betrays a fearsome will that measures itself alone against destiny, that is capable of descending into the world arena like the hero, the champion of hopeless causes. It was an action born of ambition and pride taken to the highest level. 'As the irrevocable words fell from my lips, I felt a life ending in me, the life I had led in a united France and an indivisible army. At forty-nine, I was entering into an adventure like a man whom destiny has thrown out of line.' With a

June 1940. Paris falls to the Germans

single stroke, the General was cutting himself off, for the time being at least, from his country. He was taking, for a soldier, the most serious step of all: disobedience. He found himself 'alone and stripped of everything, like a man standing at the edge of an ocean which he intends to swim.'

Finally, the call was his revenge against the 'leaders who have been, for many years, at the head of the French armies . . . ' All at once the bitterness engendered by years of incomprehension and isolation gushed forth, scarcely tempered by the bitter satisfaction of knowing that he had been right all along. De Gaulle twice recalled his role as a Cassandra and alluded to 'mechanical force'.

The Call of 18th June was a purely military appeal. At this stage, de Gaulle went no further than to place himself at the head of a band of volunteers resolved to continue the struggle under British colours. But in the days that followed, the perspective changed. Another note appeared. His tone hardened, became aggressive. The decisive turning point was 19th June. Then the Call was transformed into an indictment, a political manifesto. The repudiation of the armistice became identified with a repudiation of the new régime. The General was at pains to avoid the impression that he was acting as some sort of mercenary: 'Now that the loyalties of Frenchmen are hopelessly divided, now that the government has withered away in enemy servitude, now that our institutions are incapable of functioning, I, General de Gaulle, French soldier and leader, feel strongly that I am speaking in the name of France.' A decisive step had been taken. It was suddenly obvious that compromise was out of the question, that intransigence was total. Charles de Gaulle considered that he had placed himself at the highest level, that he had 'taken over France'.

The break with Vichy was soon complete. On 20th June, Weygand ordered General de Gaulle to return to France and the following communiqué was transmitted over the radio: 'General de Gaulle, who has spoken on the BBC, no longer belongs to the French Government and is not entitled to make public statements. His announcements should be disregarded.' After a last minute hesitation, de Gaulle refused to return to France as soon as he knew that the armistice had been accepted, an armistice which he regarded as 'not only a capitulation but an enslavement.' On 2nd August, the war tribunal at Clermont-Ferrand condemned him to death, but Pétain later wrote in the margin of the document: 'The sentence in absence can only be academic. It has never entered my mind to put it into effect.' Laval later remarked: 'You can't condemn someone to death for excess of patriotism.'

In the conflict which arose between Vichy and London, two concepts of France were involved. For Pétain France was the earth, the native soil: it was something basic. His country meant, above all, his children, those who were living and those who were suffering. And the old Marshal, with a hint of morose enjoyment, intended to remain among them and to share their tribulations. For de Gaulle, on the other hand, France was an entity, an abstraction, an eternal and immortal France fashioned by a band of heroes. It was an immense heritage and a precious trust. 'All my life,' he said later, 'I have developed a certain idea of France, inspired as much by sentiment as by reason. The emotional part of me naturally imagines France as a princess out of a fairy story or as a madonna on a fresco. I imagine her marked out for a distinguished and exceptional destiny.'

At the same time, there were two different views on the conduct of the war. As de Gaulle never ceased to

As the Germans make themselves at home in the French capital, de Gaulle is tried and condemned to death by a French war tribunal

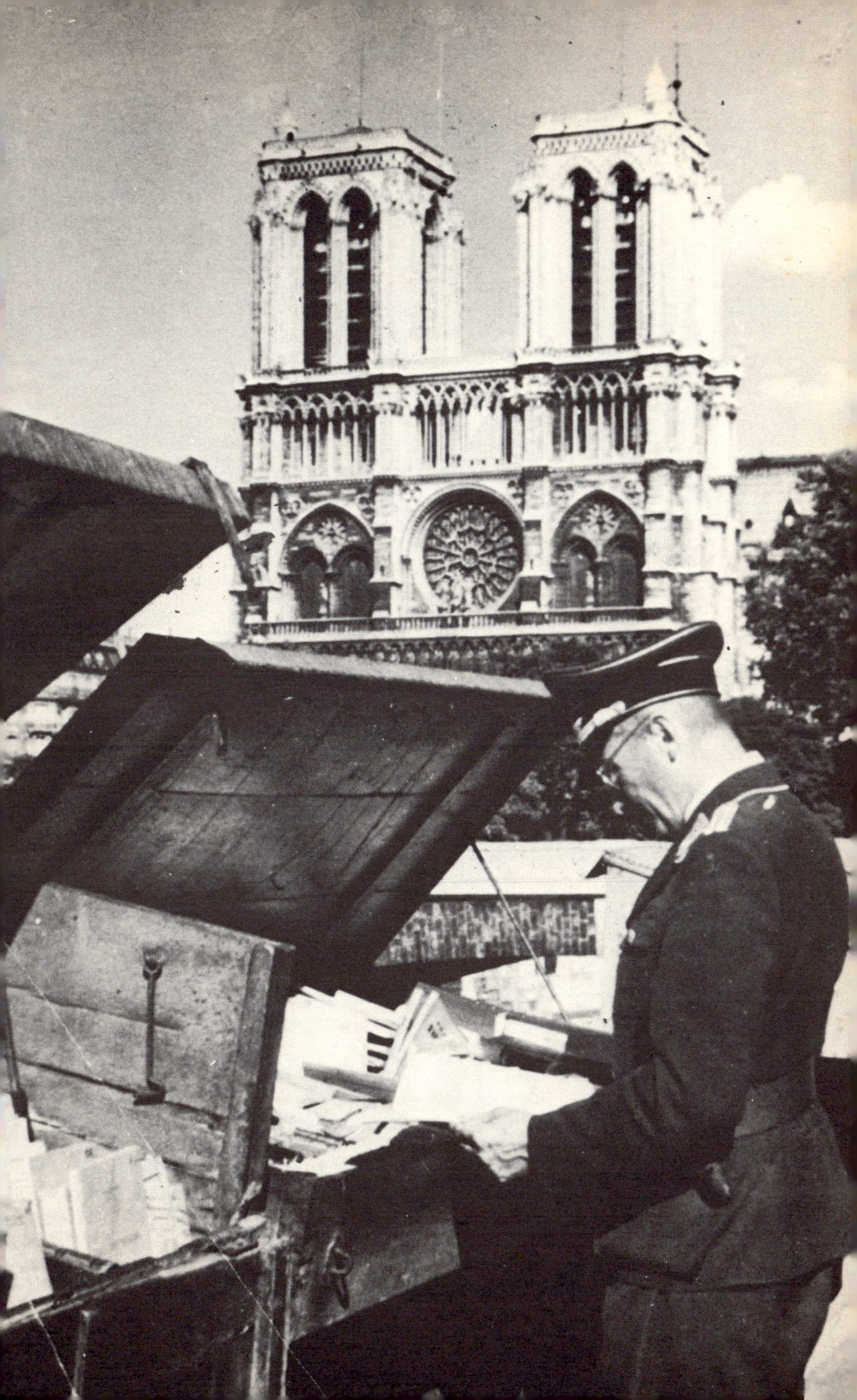

Pétain and Laval, leaders of the new Vichy regime

repeat, he believed that it was a world conflict and that 'there were immense forces which had still to be engaged.' Scarcely a fortnight after his arrival in London, he said to one of his first disciples, Maurice Schumman: 'If Hitler were going to come to London, he would be here already . . . I think that Russia will enter the war before America, but that they will both enter it . . . Hitler is thinking of the Ukraine. He will not resist the temptation to rule the destiny of Russia and it will be the beginning of his fall . . . ' It was a remarkable premonition considering the date on which it was made.

Relatively indifferent to ups and downs, romantic beneath an icy exterior, and a gambler by nature, de Gaulle remained convinced that France could participate in the war by taking up the struggle in her colonies. 'The Marshal has not understood,' he said, 'that in this war, the Mediterranean is as important as the Marne was in the last. The global aspect of the conflict totally escapes him. He says to himself: "We lost in 1870, we won in 1918 and we have lost again in 1940. It is the third round with the fourth still to come." His perspective does not go beyond the traditional Franco-German antagonism. He sees only a repetition of past conflicts.'

In reality, contrary to what de Gaulle supposed, the disagreement was not so much about the conception of the war as about the feasibility of intervention from the Empire. Pétain did not doubt the global nature of the conflict, although Russia did not enter into his calculations. In 1917, he expected 'tanks and the Americans'. In 1940, he expected the Americans and *their* tanks. But 'they will not be ready for four years,' he added. 'It will be hard and there will be bitter pills to swallow. Our agreement with the Germans is clear: *sic rebus stantibus*. After all, the conqueror always remains the arbiter . . . But in no circumstances will I declare war on the British, in no circumstances will I separate myself from the Americans.'

By nature, Pétain had a taste for temporizing and for manoeuvre in retreat. In 1914 he had declared: "The defensive becomes a necessary manoeuvre when one needs to safeguard one's troops, economize on one's potential and gain time.' While awaiting the arrival of a great American army it

Maurice Schumann, one of de Gaulle's first important recruits

would be necessary to resort to cunning and subterfuge. To maintain the Empire in the war was untimely. Great Britain could, at a push, hold out on her island, but she was not big enough to reverse the course of destiny. Pétain believed that to renounce the armistice would have been the best way to give 'the Wehrmacht the chance to celebrate Christmas at Casablanca, Algiers, Tunisia, even at Dakar and Cairo.' The old Marshal added: De Gaulle has played his hand as if he were at a poker table. That is not politics. You must examine events, X-ray them, understand them. But just to take up a position as though one were Jupiter ... it could succeed, in which case, well and good. But supposing it does not succeed. It's a game and one does not play games.'

Finally, the very nature of the defeat separated the two men. De Gaulle believed that the disaster of 1940 had arisen because those in power had resigned themselves to it, but he believed deep down that the nation remained sound and capable of the necessary effort.

For Pétain the collapse had infinitely more profound causes. These stemmed from a structual crisis whose symptoms he cited as pacifism, a falling birth rate, and a lack of drive. The defeat therefore demanded a cure: the re-establishment of order in every domain. It should be the starting point for a veritable 'National Revolution'.

Thus at the end of June 1940, the breach between Vichy and London was complete. For Pétain the watchwords were self-examination, renewal, a waiting game. For de Gaulle, the war was 'a terrible problem, but one with a solution'. The victory of the free world was not in doubt: the Empire was a trump card which should be played at once.

On this point, the debate was not without some resemblance to that between Pétain and Clémenceau in 1917-18. In the short run, the scepitcal and despairingly realist old Marshal was probably right. A lightning visit by Major General Koeltz to North Africa on the eve of the signature of the armistice showed the impossibility of serious resistance to a German attack, however weak, from Libya or Spain. The only forces in

Hitler inspects the newly-fallen capital

North Africa were mainly indigenous and had no heavy armaments. The air force was without spares and workshops. Stocks in the armament industries were insufficient or nonexistent. In 1942 it would be necessary completely to re-arm the African army. As for the navy, it had only one base worth of the name, Bizerta, half-an-hour from Sicily by air.

But, in the long term, de Gaulle's imaginative vision would prove prophetic. He believed implicitly that the armistice could only lead to a new catastrophe, that opened wide the door to compromise, surrender and total capitulation.

The General therefore meant to become the incarnation of the resistance of the ideal France, a France *en soi* in the philosophical sense of the term. His policy was mapped out in advance. Struggle against the Axis powers naturally. But behind the Call of 18th June lay two major struggles: to make himself recognized by the Free World as the only authentic spokesman for France; and 'to lead France back on to the right path', to tear the mass of the country away from the seductions of the Vichy régime and to place it back on its historical course.

Meanwhile, during the dramatic summer of 1940, it was to Marshal Pétain that the great majority of the French people turned. By vote on 10th July, Parliament accorded him full powers, with an immense majority. The Third Republic disappeared behind the French State and the slogan 'Work, Family, Fatherland' replaced 'Liberty, Equality and Fraternity'. France found herself a traditionalist, authoritarian régime which drew its inspiration from the Right and which was not dissimilar to Salazar's and Franco's states in Portugal and Spain. Under the terms of the armistice, France retained the attributes of sovereignty, a free zone,

Hitler is overcome with joy at the signing of the Armistice

an army of 100,000 men and above all two important trump cards: a colonial empire with sovereign forces and a homogenous and well-trained fleet. The Vichy Government was recognized by all the great powers, from the Soviet Union to the Vatican.

In contrast, it must be admitted that 'Free France' cut a wretched figure and that General de Gaulle's movement looked as though it might remain a minority group in the pay of Great Britain. The Call of 18th June, and the messages broadcast in the days that followed found little response among a population fleeing on the roads and shattered by a paralysing defeat. Although the Call was printed in four or five newspapers in the South of France, the messages addressed to the governor-generals of the colonies – Nogues in Morocco, Boisson in Dakar, Peyrouton in Algeria – achieved nothing: after a few hesitations the 'proconsuls' rallied to the Marshal. The attempts to rally the French who were still in Great Britain – Bethouard's Alpine division, and several warship crews – yielded only mediocre results: a few hundred soldiers and sailors, a handful of officers among whom were Lieutenant-Colonel Magrin Verneret, called Monclar, Captain Koenig, Captain Dewavrin called Passy, and Lieu-

General Nogues, Governor-General of Morocco. He ignored de Gaulle's Call of 18th June and rallied to Pétain's Vichy regime

tenant-Commander Thierry d'Agrenlieu. The biggest catch was Admiral Muselier, who had been deprived of all commands by Darlan since 1939. This scanty little group was swelled, during the month of July, by airmen and isolated individuals who, by the workings of fortune had managed to cross the channel. There were 133 fishermen from the Island of Sein who were afraid of being taken over by the Germans. At the beginning of August the Free French numbered only 7,000 in all.

Those who came over were not all soldiers. There were a certain number of civilians, mostly inclined towards the Left: Maurice Schumann, the journalist, René Cassin, professor of law, René Pleven, the banker. Pierre Cot, who was considered to be too showy, too 'Popular Front', was turned down, and other personalities like Jean Monnet, André Maurois, Alexis Léger, Henri de Kérills merely passed through London on their way to the United States.

Why were these results so disappointing? The drama at Mers-el-Kebir undoubtedly played a part in reducing

Lieutenant-Commander Thierry d'Argenlieu, French High Commissioner in the Pacific. He was one of the few high-ranking officers to respond immediately to de Gaulle's call.

recruits. General de Gaulle was at first indignant, but he ended by justifying the British action. He knew that Admiral Darlan would never have given up his 'fief'. Other factors also played a part. Most of the officers and soldiers, far from obeying entirely selfish motives, felt that their duty lay in winning back France. The Mother Country, wounded and unhappy, needed her children. Others, and by no means few, refused to enter a movement so obviously patronized by Great Britain: 'I think it would be a great mistake,' wrote Jean Monnet, 'to try to set up an organization in Great Britain which might seem to be a pole of authority created abroad under the protection of Great Britain.' Finally, the programme of renewal advertised by Pétain had its appeal. For many, the London movement looked like being the retreat of the most questionable elements of the Third Republic. Indeed, here was an undoubtedly weak spot for the Free French. Among the eighty deputies and senators who voted 'no' on the 10th day of July 1940, only a weak minority had condemned the armistice. Most of them were voting against the extinction of republican institutions, against a measure granting full powers to one man, however prestigious he might be.

For the British, the embryonic nature of de Gualle's movement was an undeniable disappointment. They could no longer hope that leading personalities like Paul Reynaud, Edouard Herriot, or Georges Mandel would come over. But in spite of all this, Churchill agreed on 7th August to conclude a limited agreement with de Gaulle in the form of an exchange of letters. The General was recognized as 'Leader of all the Free French, wherever they may be' – a skilfully chosen title. 'The Free French force' would continue to fight in close liaison with the British armies. Their expenses, as well as those of the 'civilian body', would be paid by the British Treasury and would be reimbursed at the end of the war. Besides this, Great Britain promised 'full restoration of the independence and grandeur of France'. It was specified that the Free French could not take up arms against France. Nevertheless, a secret letter corrected a part of this last provision: only 'a France not subject to direct or indirect constraint from Germany' would be safe from attack. Finally, Churchill refused to undertake to restore France to her full territorial integrity.

In spite of all this, the agreement was of paramount importance. It was the birth certificate of Free France, documenting her arrival on the international stage. It was de Gaulle's first attempt, although a limited one, at talking with Great Britain as 'one power to another'.

Some of the 133 fishermen from the Island of Sein who crossed the Channel to swell de Gaulle's tiny force

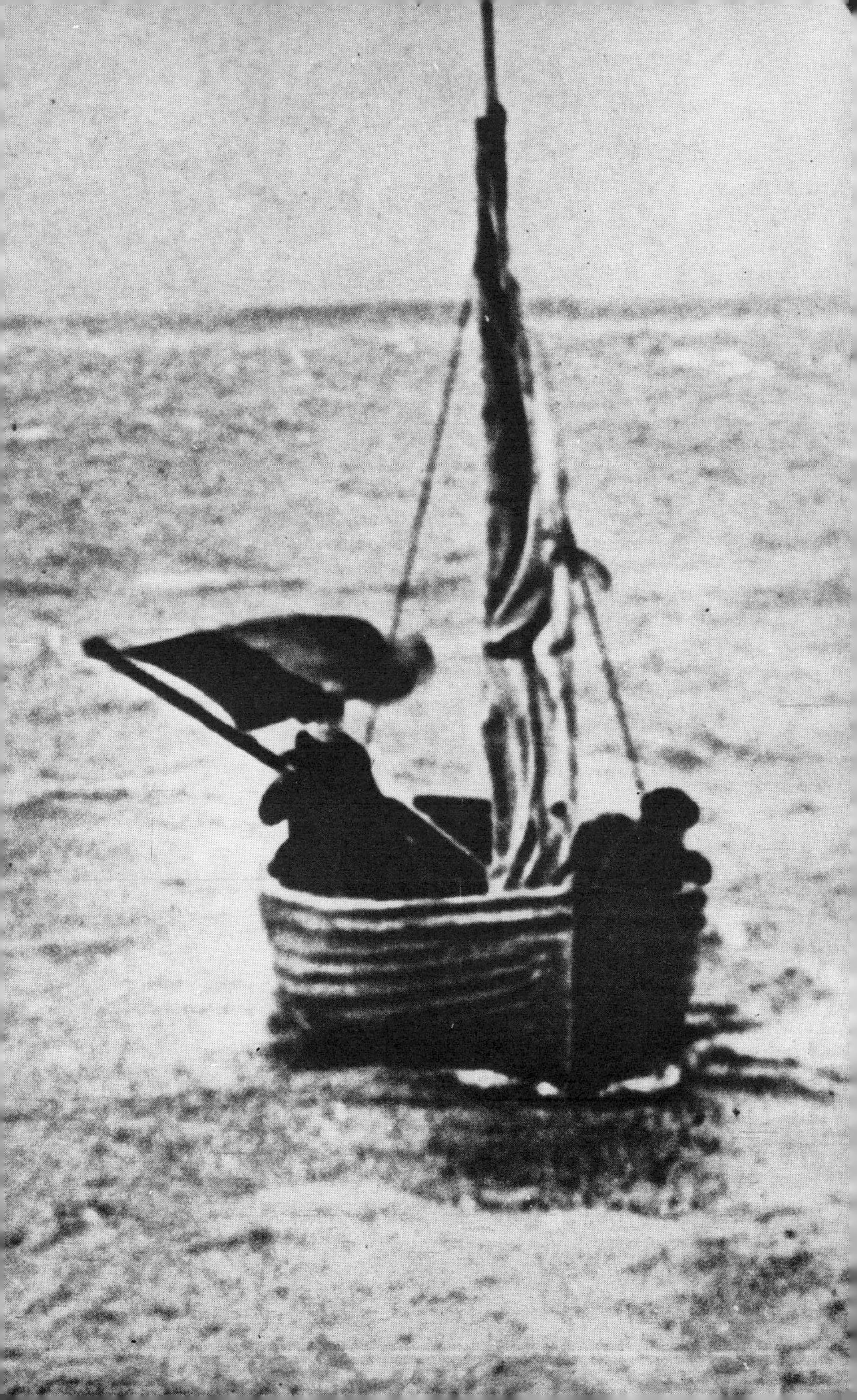

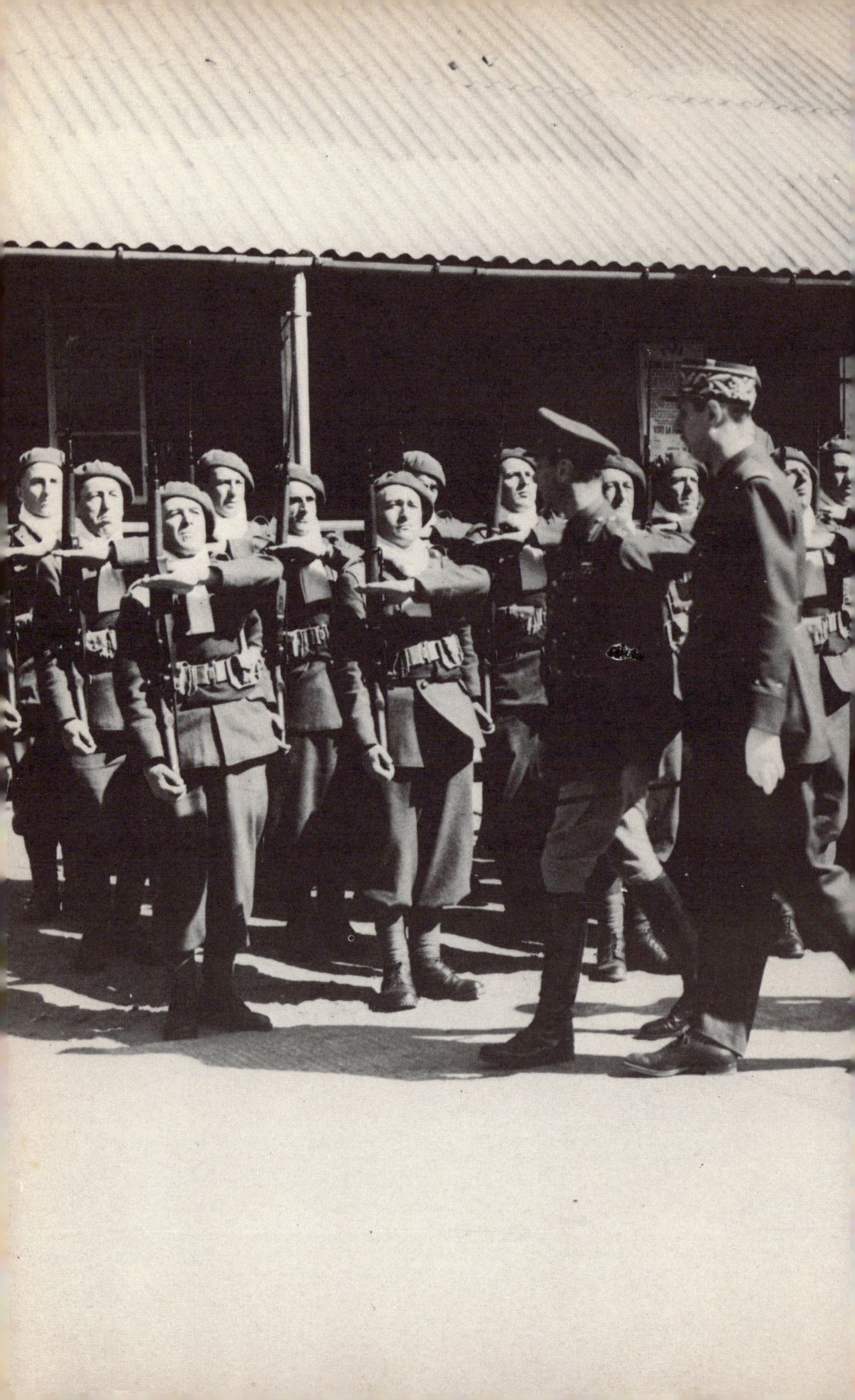

Drama at Dakar

At the end of the first year de Gaulle could draw up a balance sheet, still modest, of his activities. On the credit side he could chalk up a certain degree of recognition and some troops. They were few, admittedly, but they were ardent. On 14th July King George VI agreed to review them. On the way out of the ceremony de Gaulle could not help remarking: 'My God, how short my sword is!' But at least it was there. For the time being the essential problem was to ensure himself a territorial base. The General ardently wished to escape the servitude of exile in a foreign land. And, during the month of August a first ray of light, although still a weak one, pierced the gloom. The governor of the colony of Chad, a negro by the name of Félix Eboué, rallied to de Gaulle. The general seized his chance. He sent a small group of resolute and determined men to Chad: Commander Philippe de Hauteclocque (Leclerc), René Pleven, Commander Ornano and Colonel de Larminat. The results were promising. In a matter of days, the Cameroons, and all French Equitorial Africa, with the exception of the Gabon, broke away from Vichy and, following the example of Chad, rallied to the Cross of Lorraine. Most of the Pacific possessions and the Indian stations joined this territorial group.

De Gaulle intended to exploit this advantage at once and to enlarge the breach which was appearing in the colonial empire, till then wholly faithful to Vichy. Fort Lamy, Douala, Brazzaville were insufficient as political and strategic bases. Certainly they were in the heart of immense territories, but these were sparsely populated. Dakar was the prize which had to be won. If this great Atlantic port rallied to the Free French it would provoke a tremor capable of drawing the whole Empire into the war, including North Africa. In Dakar, the Free French would at last find the capital in keeping with their political ambitions.

De Gaulle imparted his plans to his general staff. 'If we are to represent the interests of our country in a worthy manner, both in the eyes of our allies and of Frenchmen in France and abroad who support our cause, it is of extreme importance that the seat of the French government which is carrying on the struggle should be situated on French soil. We cannot, of

King George VI reviews Free French troops, August 1940

course, install ourselves at the antipodes, for we must remain in the centre of the action; equally the government must be in a city which, by its size and its renown ineluctably attracts the crystallization of what is and remains French... That is why I have decided – and my information shows that it is possible – to establish at Dakar the capital of the Empire at war.'

De Gaulle told Churchill of this plan. After some hesitation the British Premier agreed to sponsor the operation. An engagement at Dakar would have many advantages for Great Britain, if only that it would prevent Germany from using the port one day for refuelling her U-Boats and surface ships engaged in the Battle of the Atlantic. The Prime Minister's imaginative mind immediately pictured a scene: 'Dakar awakes one morning, sorrowful and uncertain. Then, in the rising sun, the inhabitants see the sea covered afar off with ships. An immense fleet, 100 vessels, both warships and cargo ships. Slowly they draw near signalling on the radio ... messages of friendship... Then an inoffensive little boat breaks loose

Félix Eboué, Governor of Chad. When he rallied to de Gaulle most of French Equatorial Africa followed suit

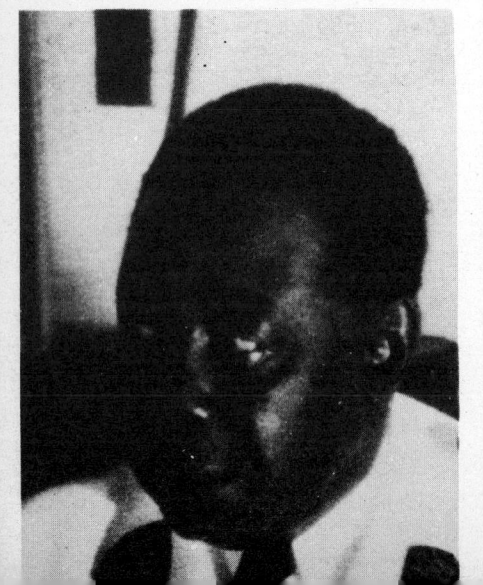

Admiral Cunningham, commander of expedition 'Menace' against Dakar

from them bearing the white flag of truce...'

Expedition *Menace*, commanded by Admiral Cunningham, arrived at Dakar on 23rd September. It comprised a powerful British squadron with the aircraft carrier *Ark Royal*, the battleships *Barham* and *Resolution*, several cruisers and a few small French vessels. De Gaulle himself was taking part in the exercise, on board the Dutch ship *Westerland*, showing French colours. In the end, the British had opted for direct action, dropping de Gaulle's plan which called for a landing at Conakry and a march by land to Dakar, which would perhaps have allowed the Gaullist elements to steal the limelight.

It is not necessary to tell the story of the Dakar affair blow by blow but simply to recall the reasons for a resounding Allied defeat. Firstly, the affair was badly organized and secrecy was not respected as well as it might have been. Then, when the squadron arrived at Dakar on the morning of 23rd September a thick mist concealed the port and the town. The expected theatrical effect was completely lacking. The Free French and the British then committed a grave

A convoy arrives at Dakar from Britain. De Gaulle hoped that if this great Atlantic port fell to the Free French then the whole French Empire would be drawn into the war

psychological error. The radio announcement said that the Allied forces were intervening in Dakar to defend the garrison and its population against the Germans, but there was not one member of the Wehrmacht in Dakar and the armistice commission had not even arrived. In any case, the operation took place too late. For the Governor, General Boisson and for the army and navy, the time for hesitation had passed. The instructions sent by Vichy had managed to convince those in charge that only the 'loyalty' of the colonies would allow France to avoid complete servitude and a fate similar to that of Poland.

Finally, in estimating the number of his supporters in Dakar at forty per cent de Gaulle was making a bad mistake. The few movements organized among the people or the initiatives taken by certain groups would have been easily neutralized. In fact a strong anti-British and anti-Gaullist feeling existed in the army and particularly in the navy. Many of the men had never forgiven de Gaulle for his final endorsement of Mers-el-Kebir. And the attacks launched at Dakar itself on 8th July, as part of Operation 'Catapult', against the battleship *Richelieu* had left a deep impression.

On the morning of the first day the British remained in the background while de Gaulle tried to obtain support without bloodshed. But there was little response to his call and his emissaries were captured at Rufisque airport and even machine-gunned in the port. D'Argenlieu and Bécourt-Foch were seriously wounded. For the first time since the revolution, Frenchmen had spilt French blood and this would cause lasting resentment on both sides.

After the defeat of the Free French the British decided to take the matter into their own hands. Two days of violent fighting ensued. There was an abortive landing at Rufisque, but the main part of the action consisted of an artillery duel between the British ships and the French vessels moored in the roads, supported by a few cannons on shore. The *Richelieu* and Admiral Bourrague's three cruisers which had come to reinforce Dakar a few days before the beginning of the expedition, replied fiercely to the British firing. Finally, on 25th September, because of the damage suffered by his vessels and in accordance with Churchill's wishes, Admiral Cunningham decided to give up the expedition. The battleship *Barham* was bracketed several times, the *Resolution* was foundering after being torpedoed by the submarine *Beveziers* and had to be taken under tow, and several planes from the *Ark Royal* were destroyed.

For de Gaulle, the blow was particularly harsh. Both in London and Washington his reputation was seriously damaged. There was a storm of sarcasm. For the first time, he had been the cause of a fratricidal fight between Frenchmen. The realization of what he had done had a profound psychological effect on de Gaulle. For forty-eight hours he locked himself in his cabin, refusing to see anyone. 'After Dakar he was never the same man. He was never happy again', said one of those who knew him best. But it was too late to retreat. The point of no return was far behind him. A new initiative was called for. The General could not continue to vacillate between adventure and politics.

Having failed to find a capital worthy of the name, the leader of the Free French decided, in spite of everything, to emphasize the political nature of his movement and to rid himself of too military an appearance. It was thus that he prepared to lay the

General Boisson, the pro-Vichy Governor of Dakar

General Catroux, former Governor of Indo-China and a most important adherent to the Free French cause

foundations of a real government.

After the Dakar fiasco, he decided to take possession of his 'domain'. In turn he visited Douala, Fort Lamy, and Brazzaville. He then gave the order to embark upon the conquest of the Gabon, an order which would only be executed with further internecine bloodshed. His stay in Africa was marked by several conversions to his cause, among them General Catroux. The Governor of Indo-China had just been *stellenbosched* by Vichy for having shown weakness in the face of the Japanese demands. Feeling lost and adrift, Catroux hesitated to return to France. He wandered to London, then to Cairo and finally decided in spite of his five stars, to place himself under de Gaulle's orders, For the leader of the Free French, this support was an asset of the utmost importance. It confirmed the political nature of his mission and sanctioned his claim to play the role of head of state: 'From the time Catroux came over, de Gaulle was no longer bound by ranks but invested with a duty beyond iherarchy.'

Strengthened in this way, de Gaulle

Above: A poster proclaims Dakar's sympathy with Vichy. *Below:* The French battleship *Richelieu*. Vichy resistance was fierce and the British expedition was a fiasco. De Gaulle had seriously overestimated the strength of his support in Dakar

Above left: Pleven, responsible for Finance and the Colonies in de Gaulle's government-in-exile, the National Committee. *Above right:* Maurice Dejean, National Committee member responsible for Foreign Affairs. *Below:* De Gaulle and Leclerc in Douala

René Cassin, responsible for Justice and Education

Admiral Muselier, responsible for the Navy

was able to create a 'Defence Council' at Brazzaville, embryo of a real government, and appoint Catroux to it. The decision to set up a new organ with an appearance of legitimacy was precipitated by two events: De Gaulle had been warned that Weygand and Noguès might possibly break away from Vichy and he wanted to cover himself against every contingency. Then, the interview between Pétain and Hitler at Montoire, followed by the announcement that they would adopt a policy of 'collaboration', gave him the chance of finally contesting the legitimacy of the Vichy régime and of proclaiming himself the sole protector of French interests.

From then on, for the French people, there was only one legitimate authority; his own. He now believed that all France was invested in him.

De Gaulle did not prolong his stay in Brazzaville. In October he returned to London, an event which had the effect of 'paving over a pond jumping with frogs'. The atmosphere among the Free French in London was like that of a small Italian court during the Renaissance, flourishing with the worst intrigues. De Gaulle made every effort to enforce some sort of order in this bear garden. For the time being, his aim was to create an organization comparable to the governments in exile of the Netherlands, Belgium or Norway. The Defence Council of the Empire was failing to function properly because of the absence of its members, and to make good this defect the General created a Military Committee, over which he himself presided. He also convened an administrative congress which regrouped the civil services into four main categories: administrative and financial affairs, foreign and economic affairs, political affairs, and justice. But the most important step was taken with the 'Order' of 24th September 1941 which instituted a National Committee entitled to legislate 'until such time as a body of the French people shall be constituted with the power to express the national will independent of the enemy.' Meanwhile measures were taken to set up 'a Consultative Assembly intended to provide the National Committee with as great an expression as possible of

Above: 'He has literally taken upon himself his country's dishonour, like Christ took on the sins of the world for the Christian faith'. *Below:* Members of the Free French at work in their HQ in Carlton Gardens, London

the public opinion.'

Headed by de Gaulle, the Committee included Pléven, responsible for Finance and the Colonies, Maurice Dejean responsible for Foreign Affairs, René Cassin responsible for the departments of justice and education, Diethlem for the Interior, Labour and Information, General Legentilhomme for war, and Admiral Muselier for the navy. Even though the powers of the commissioners for Civil Affairs – it was not yet a question of ministers – extended no further than their own offices, the Free French nevertheless had their own government based on the model of the cabinets of the 3rd Republic. But it was still only a democratic façade, in spite of the legal efforts of people like Professor Cassin. De Gaulle behaved like an autocrat, a prince, with the same disregard for democratic rules as the Marshal in Vichy. He alone appointed the commissioners. At the meetings of the Committee, there was merely an exchange of views; no one voted. René Cassin normally synthesized the views expressed, but only the General made the decisions.

This dictatorial behaviour earned

Charles and Madame de Gaulle relax in their Hertfordshire cottage

de Gaulle the hostility of a small group of Frenchmen who had fled to London but who refused to join the Free French. They were intransigent republicans like Pierre Comert and Georges Gombault or journalists like André Labarthe and Raymond Aron. They did not hesitate to treat de Gaulle as a royalist and a clerical: they dubbed him 'General de Gauleiter'. Their attacks were directed above all at his entourage, in particular Colonel Remy, head of the famous information bureau, the BCRA. Insinuations were made about this 'mini Gestapo' led by an emulator of Himmler, suggesting that the 'clan 93' – as the government was termed – went in for torture.

De Gaulle appeared to be indifferent to these calumnies. He played the role of a distant and inaccessible master over his little flock of exiles. He believed that such a role was in keeping with the circumstances. At the beginning, he consented to greet personally all the new members of the Free French, in the building that had been placed at his disposal in Carlton Gardens. But more often than not the welcome was icy. The General asked questions, listened to his interlocutor, proposed an assignment. Then he would get up, clumsily straightening his immense body, take a few steps, smile vaguely and shake hands. The door would close and the visitor make his way out, astonished and disappointed. Sometimes, with a few of his 'friends', smoking cigarette after cigarette, de Gaulle would let himself go and talk about the war, and about France's place in the world after victory. But they were monologues, not conversations. Jokes and outbursts of humour were so rare as to be almost non-existent. Even with those with whom he worked every day de Gaulle never relaxed, never let himself go. During his exile in London his mask was seen to fall only once. When the sortie from Bir Hakim was announced, Charles de Gaulle shed tears of joy.

His rare moments of relaxation were at the weekends when he joined his family in their cottage on the outskirts of London. Even this was marred because he was constantly worried about the poor health of his daughter Anne. For propaganda reasons a British photographer was sent to film the family life of the General and his wife. De Gaulle protested at this publicity: 'Churchill wants to launch me like a new brand of soap'. The image that the viewer

French sailors in London buy 'France'

retains from this film of the de Gaulle family is that of a simple and devoted wife who knew how to fade into the background behind this immense, strange and gauche man, with his awkward smile and a screen appearance which inspired both amusement and respect.

As time passed de Gaulle grew more distant, more impenetrable and more glacial than ever. But his bearing, his intransigence, his avoidance of anything which would seem like weakness or compromise were all important to his role as saviour of a wounded country, a country that had been humiliated and, for the time being, beaten. General Spears' wife wrote: 'I think that he feels the dishonour of France with an intensity of which few men are capable, and that he has literally taken upon himself his country's dishonour, like Christ took on the sins of the world for the Christian faith.

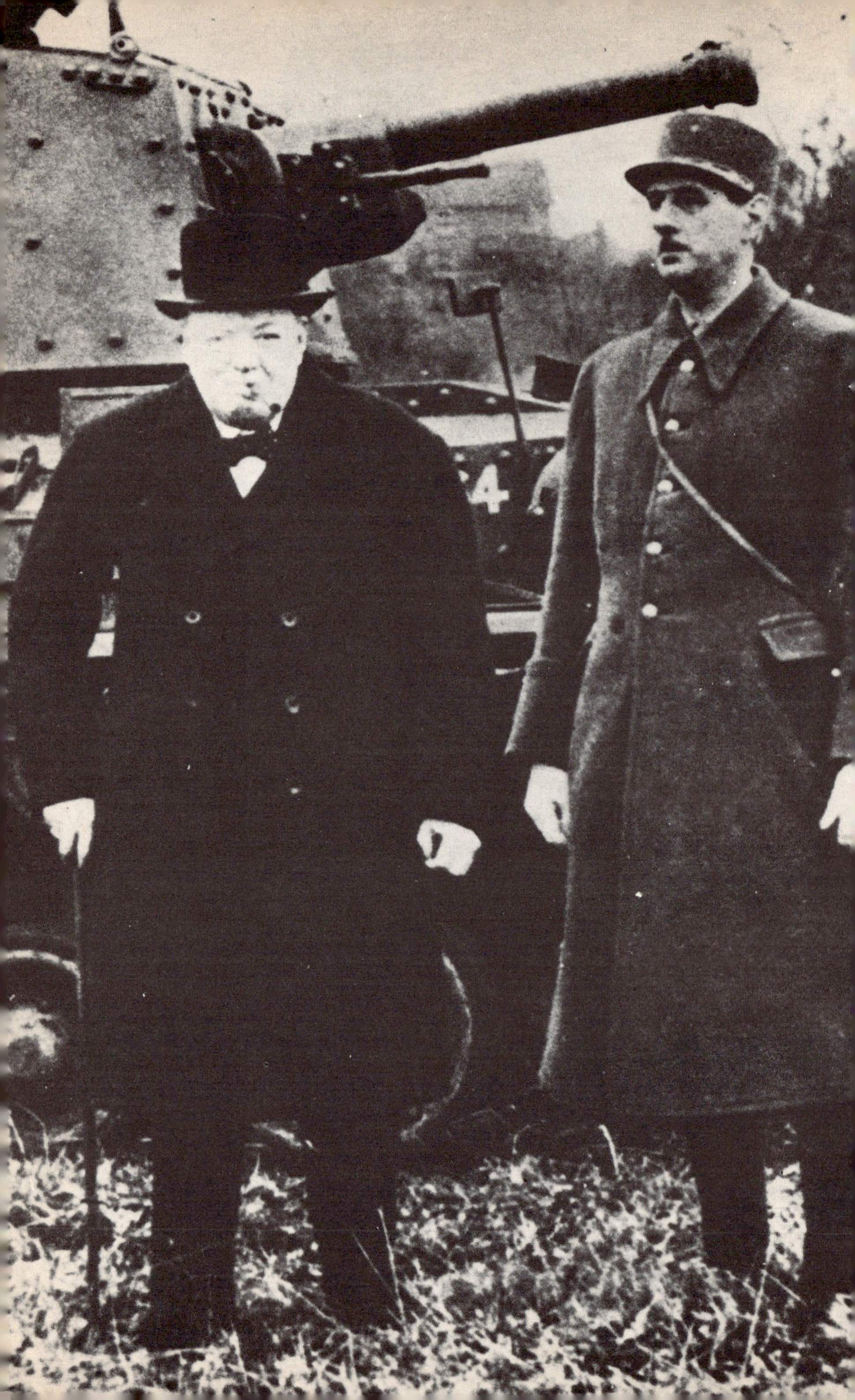

Conflict with the Allies

In his vision of himself as France's messiah lies the key to his stormy and tumultuous behaviour towards the Allies. It was not long before de Gaulle was, in effect, more at war with the British than with the Germans. 'I bear the burden of France's interests and of her destiny,' he liked to say. 'It is too heavy and I am too weak to stoop. For in the extremity to which France is reduced there can be neither compromise nor any fair dealings.' De Gaulle did not intend to be a pawn in the hands of the Allies and of Great Britain in particular. Sentiment and reason alike bade him repudiate defeat and the armistice, and he aimed to be treated as an authentic head of state, as an equal, as the sole trustee of French legitimacy. British reluctance to consider him as the true representative of France caused him intense frustration. While the governments-in-exile sent letters of recognition to Carlton Gardens from October 1941, the British and United States Governments spoke only of a 'National Free Committee'.

Furthermore, the suspicion and mistrust with which he was regarded hurt the General to the quick. He

Churchill and de Gaulle in March 1941

remained convinced, and not always without reason, that while Great Britain was engaged in a fight to the death with the Axis powers, she was nevertheless pursuing her traditional colonial ambitions and that the French defeat could only supply the opportunity for her to add to her empire. De Gaulle had been brought up on history, convinced that 'the sword is the axis of the world', and he remained confident that the alliance of the democratic nations against the totalitarian powers was temporary and that victory would herald the return of traditional struggles for colonial influence. This conviction explains the General's frequently disconcerting politics. For de Gaulle, France still had the potential of a great power, and he believed that she was only *temporarily* beaten. As guarantor of her interests, he had to reserve a place for her on the day of reckoning and to forestall the ambitions of the Anglo-Saxon powers which were 'in the nature of things'. 'We are in the midst of foreigners,' he declared. 'For the Allies are strangers. Tomorrow they could become enemies . . .'

It was with Félix Gouin, when he arrived in London, that de Gaulle was most explicit about his conception of the relationship between the Free French and her powerful partners. Gouin asked the General if rumours of grave differences of opinion between himself and Churchill were true and records that as de Gaulle prepared to answer, his 'marmoreal face darkened, a slight shadow descended on his brow, and he answered my questions in a grave voice. "Yes," he told me, "our British friends are not always easy to get on with. You know them, but I think that I know them a great deal better than most of our countrymen. The fight to the death they are at present waging against the Reich aggravates that ruthless love of power which is the dominant characteristic of their race. That is, no doubt, what causes them to forget, even encroach on others' interests and think only of their own."

The General stopped for a few moments; his hands were shaking slightly, his expression brightened and from his lips fell those astonishing words which still ring in my ears and which are without doubt the key to the psychology of this outstanding personality: "You see," he said, "my duty is straightforward. Until the victory, I am accountable for what makes France a great people and a great country. I will surrender none of those elements which go to make this greatness. And the weaker I become" – he hammered the point home in a voice suddenly harsh – "the more intransigent will I be to defend our rights and make them respected . . . What would have become of the fatherland," he added, "if Joan of Arc, Danton, Clémenceau had wanted to compromise?"'

His singlemindedness could be said to justify to some extent the constant distrust with which he regarded the 'dark designs' of London and Washington and the see-saw politics that had been practised since 1941 in the flirt with Moscow. At the beginning of 1943, de Gaulle declared to General Bouscat: 'I do not want a policy of alliances which commit us once and for all. I want France to play a balancing game in the world, leaning first towards Russia then towards Britain and so on. France should find her own way, and make herself a place in the world with her own resources.'

Meanwhile, the General's behaviour irritated and annoyed the British. Certainly, everyone respected of his patriotism; they understood his sufferings, his hurt pride and even his touchy vanity. Commander Alec Lacy, liaison officer of the Royal Navy to the General, said: 'Charles de Gaulle is the most determined, the most proud, the most intransigent, the most obstinate, the most ruthless, but also the most brilliant leader that I have ever met.' Churchill, too, paid homage to the leader of the Free French: 'I had continuous difficulties and many sharp antagonisms with him. There was, however, a dominant element in our relationship. I could not regard him as representing captive and prostrate France, nor indeed the France that had a right to decide freely the future for herself. I knew he was no friend of England. But I always recognised in him the spirit and conception which, across the pages of history, the word "France" would ever proclaim. I understood and admired, while I resented, his arrogant demeanour. Here he was – a refugee, an exile from his country under sentence of death, in a position entirely dependent upon the goodwill of the British Government, and also now of the United States. The Germans had conquered his country. He had no real foothold anywhere. Never mind, he defied all. Always, even when he was at his most irritating, he seemed to express the character of France, a Great Nation, with all its pride, its authority, its ambition.'

Nevertheless, de Gaulle's pretensions to be the sole incarnation of France, his wounding remarks, his

Félix Gouin, the man to whom de Gaulle confided his distrust of the British and Americans

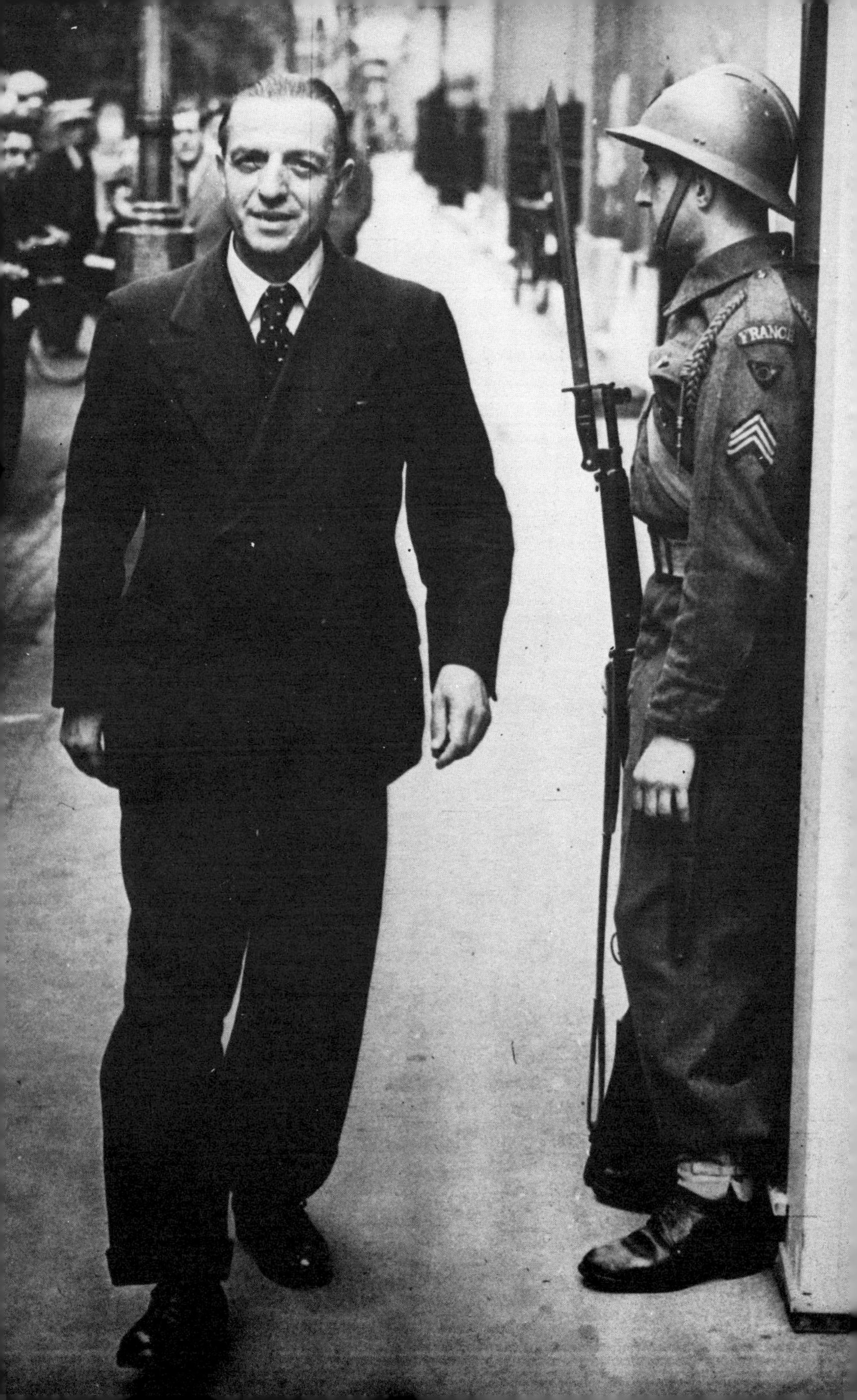

De Gaulle speaks at a factory in London

noisy and often maladroit declarations, antagonized the Anglo-Saxons he so distrusted. To pragmatic minds the behaviour of 'Frankenstein' seemed on occasions to approach the realms of pathology. Did he not consider himself the living replica of Joan of Arc? His insistence on representing the interests of France when he had only a symbolic military force seemed both grotesque and provocative. People began to wonder whether he was not, after all, following purely personal motives. His clashes with Churchill were constant and the British Prime Minister one day snapped that of all the crosses he had had to bear the Cross of Lorraine was the heaviest. The conflict was further complicated by a personality clash. The two leaders were as romantic and as passionate as the other. But Churchill's expansiveness and truculence clashed with the coldness of the Frenchman wrapped in his wounded dignity and icy exterior.

The Free French had many setbacks in store for them. Those who came over to them were fewer than they expected and they suffered from the aftermath of the Dakar affair, which had widened the rift between de Gaulle and Churchill. The British felt that the rashness of the Free French had largely been the cause of the disaster and they remembered the ostentatious purchases of tropical clothes in Lon-

personage had sent the following message to a Vichy minister: 'De Gaulle is annoying us. He thinks he is Joan of Arc. OK. We are going to burn him. There is no need for a stake as there was in 1431. All we need do is inform the Vichy government of the day and time of his next flight plan to the Near-East, to give them the flight plan . . . ' It seems that the Marshal replied: 'Let the English do their own dirty work.'

Whatever the truth behind these '*combinazioni*', the fact remains that Churchill had to consider the situation from the two different standpoints. Apart from the moral capital of the Gaullist movement in an ideological struggle, all the Free French had to offer was a mere handful of men. It was true that Equitorial Africa now provided an aerial bridge between Nigeria and the Sudan, but, on a purely strategic level, it was the Vichy government who held all the trump cards for France at the time, including the navy and the Empire.

In October 1940, after Dakar and at the time of Montoire, Churchill agreed to receive an emissary from Marshal Pétain, Professor Rougier. After lengthy discussions, an agreement was sealed by which Vichy undertook to do nothing that would directly help the Axis. In return, the British Government agreed to lift the blockade, to mute the attacks made by the BBC on the Marshal's government and above all to stop inciting the French colonies to revolt. At the same time, King George VI sent a secret concillatory letter to Pétain.

In spite of this, the relationship between Churchill and de Gaulle was marked by a certain measure of respect and mutual consideration. On several occasions Churchill invited the General to spend the weekend at his country house, Chequers. It was one Sunday, at two o'clock in the morning, that he came in to wake his guest. 'He came in in his dressing gown, radiant with joy, de Gaulle remembered, 'a cigar in the corner of

don, and toasts 'to Dakar' drunk by certain hot-heads in pubs. In the summer of 1940 Churchill began to look round for a partner who would be easier to deal with than de Gaulle. He sounded out Catroux and Muselier, and for a long time kept hoping that he would attract the support of men like Weygand or General La Laurencie.

At the height of the tension between Great Britain and the Free French, it seemed that the British contemplated sending de Gaulle to the Isle of Man. Certain circles would even have envisaged getting rid of him, using Vichy as the intermediary. In 1945, Pétain revealed – and this was substantiated later by General Hering – that an important British

his mouth and a piece of paper in his hand.' He sat down on the edge of the General's bed and told him that the United States were going to pass the Lend-Lease Bill.'

The most serious clashes between the Free French and the British Government came in 1941-42, over Syria, Djibouti and Madagascar. De Gaulle had shown great interest in the French Mandates in the Levant ever since his arrival in London in 1940 and he had sent a message to the Governor, General Puaux. The message was never answered. Finally, in the autumn of 1940, the General sent Catroux to Cairo, to observe the situation on the spot as Free French delegate to the Middle East. On two occasions Catroux attempted to win over the Lebanon and Syria. First he tried Puaux and then his successor, General Dentz. But there was no response to his appeals. 'Syria,' he said, 'is a bitter fruit which refuses to ripen. I fear that we shall only take it by force . . .'

There were several reasons for de Gaulle's special interest in the Levant. The first was purely sentimental: it was the only French colonial territory that the General really knew, for he had spent two years with the General Staff in Beirut. If Syria and the Lebanon came over to him, it would not only strengthen his prestige but would also bring him the considerable advantage of a small army of 35,000 men who had been organised in 1939 under Weygand's command in an attempt to renew the Salonika operation of 1917-18, with the assistance of the Balkan states. Secondly, de Gaulle could not ignore the strategic value of this region which was the focal point of the Middle East. In the hands of the Axis forces, Syria would represent a grave menace to the Suez Canal and the Allies' oil supplies.

De Gaulle decorates a member of the Free French forces at Wellington barracks, London

General Dentz, French C-in-C in Syria. He resisted Catroux's efforts to persuade him to join de Gaulle

The failure to bring Syria round by persuasion forced de Gaulle to consider, at the end of 1940, a powerful operation with the 1st Free French Division under General Legentilhomme stationed in Palestine. The problem was broached by the Empire Defence Council on 3rd March 1941. It was hoped that the arrival of Gaullist forces in Syria might provoke an immediate desertion of General Dentz's troops. But the Free French had to be prepared for a bloody encounter and with less than 2,000 men, a dozen tanks and a few guns at their disposal, they could not hope to defeat the Vichy troops. For this reason British support was indispensable.

During the meeting of the Defence Committee, Leclerc and Larminat did not hide their opposition to a new battle between Frenchmen, after the lesson of Dakar. Catroux and Muselier were hesitant. Only de Gaulle and the 'civilians' were in favour of a new confrontation, and the British had still to be convinced. Churchill and Wavell remained reticent until the spring, Churchill for political reasons – he had to consider the Rougier agreements – and Wavell, Commander-in-Chief for the Middle East, for purely strategic reasons – his resources were limited and badly needed in Egypt and Greece.

But in the spring of 1941, two events completely changed the picture and gave de Gaulle a chance to attain his objective. There was a new demonstration of the lightning war and the British troops were obliged to reembark hastily for the Balkans. In May, Student's paratroops took Crete like pirates boarding a ship. This new British defeat was accompanied by serious losses, particularly in the Royal Navy which was working at full capacity in the evacuation battle.

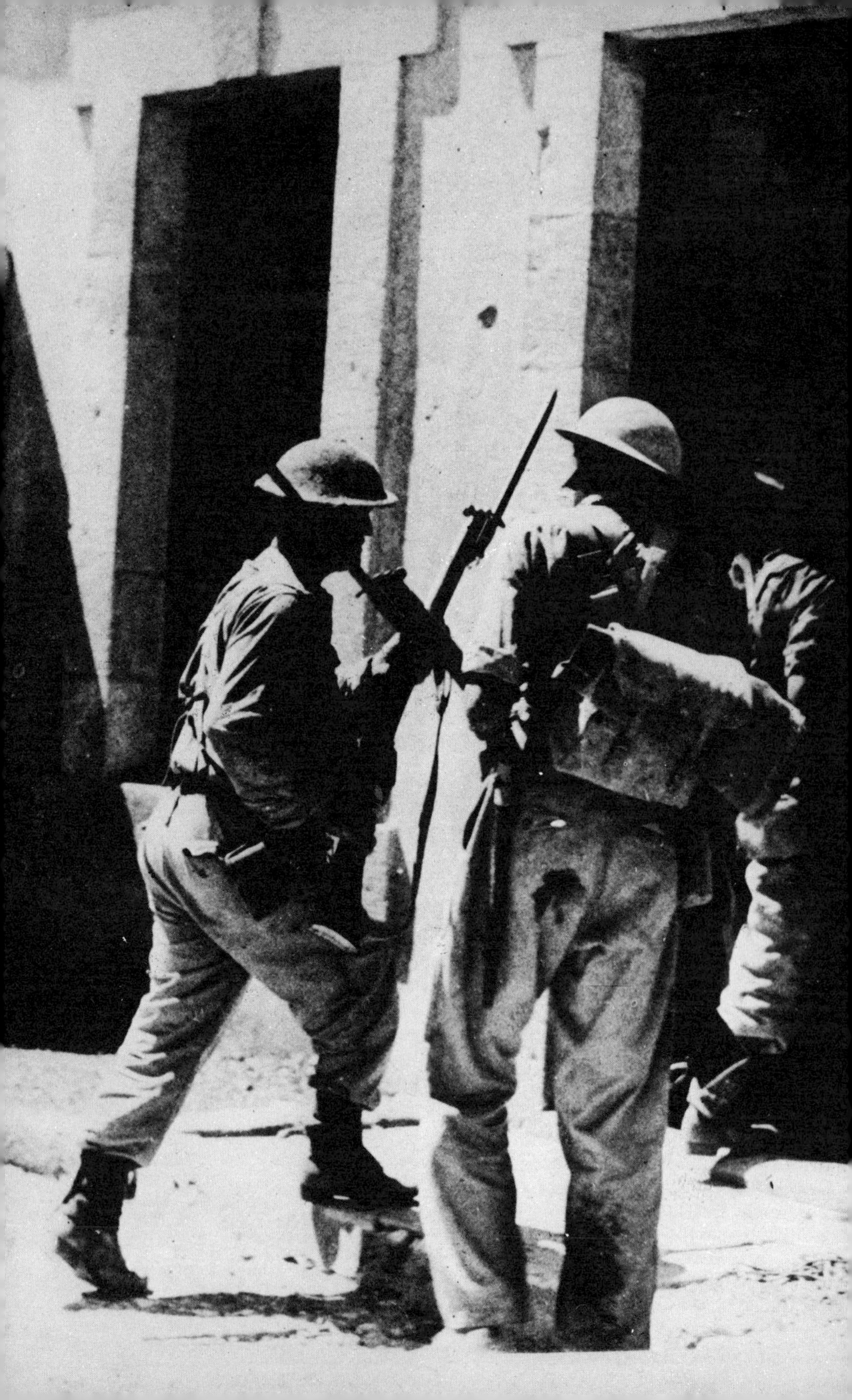

Now the war shifted to the Eastern Mediterranean. Great Britain's situation was worsened by Rachid Ali's uprising in Iraq, which naturally benefited the Axis powers. It was then that the famous 'Paris Protocols' were signed, which seemed to put Vichy France on the road to military collaboration with the Third Reich. Darlan was then at the head of the government after Laval's departure in December 1940. Without having any particular sympathy towards Germany, the Admiral no longer believed Great Britain to be capable of prolonged resistance. As the situation evolved, Darlan felt that France should obtain guarantees from the Reich about her future and a relaxation of the conditions of the armistice in return for increased 'collaboration'.

In fact, the interview between Hitler and Darlan on 12th May at Berchtesgaden was only partly successful. The Führer was visibly preoccupied with other matters – Rudolf Hess's escapade and preparations for the attack against Russia. He refused to burden himself with any obligations concerning France's future in the 'New Europe'. Her fate would depend entirely upon the magnitude of the assistance that she would give the Axis powers to help them win the war. It would be 'one good turn for another'.

The agreements concluded in Paris a few days later, envisaged, or rather confirmed, that Alep airfield in Syria would be placed at the disposal of the Luftwaffe to help the new Iraqi régime and that the port of Bizerta could be used as a logistic base for Afrika Korps. In return, France obtained a relaxation of the terms of the armistice, the release of several thousand prisoners, including military specialists like General Juin, and the possibility of re-arming a certain number of her warships.

Besides this, a supplementary protocol provided for the eventual use of

Free French forces in action against Dentz's Vichy troops in Syria

General Legentilhomme, commander of the 1st Free French Division stationed in Palestine

Dakar by Germany as a fuelling base. In return for this Darlan hoped to obtain a complete abrogation of the armistice. The Reich should, in fact, give the French Government, 'through political and economic concessions, the means to justify to her public opinion the possibility of armed conflict against Great Britain and the United States.'

In the event, this policy did not last long. Whether for Berlin or for Vichy, the price seemed too high. Summoned by Pétain, the governors of the colonies like Boisson and Noguès, supported by Weygand, formally opposed any military collaboration which might lead to a war against the Allies and the possibility of according 'facilities' to the Germans at Dakar. They believed that this would provoke a break-away of the Empire.

In the end, the Paris agreements remained dead letters and marked the end of a policy of collaboration based on reciprocal arrangements. Moreover, neither the intervention of the Luftwaffe in Syria nor the sale of arms taken from the armistice stocks could

Wounded Vichy prisoners move back from the front line during the Allied advance in Syria

prevent the collapse of the Iraqi revolt at the end of May.

But this handful of events played a decisive role. The Paris agreements and the role of the Luftwaffe in Syria put paid to British hesitations and Wavell was invited, in spite of his reluctance, to prepare an expedition against Syria and the Lebanon. On 8th June, British troops and a few batallions of Free French under the command of General Wilson crossed the frontier. It was the beginning of a fierce battle which was to last for more than a month.

Yet again, the Free French and the British committed a grave psychological error. In return for support, they promised both Lebanon and Syria their independence. There was little response. On the whole, the sympathies of the Arab nationalists lay with the Axis; for months they had been making swastika flags in the *souks* of Damascus.

On the whole, General Dentz fought a defensive battle except for a brutal counterattack which forced the British to send for reinforcements. On this occasion, General Legentilhomme's division suffered heavy losses. When fighting ceased in mid-July, 1,100 Vichy soldiers had been killed and 650 Free French. General de Gaulle later wrote: 'The ambiguity created by Vichy had to be cut out with the sword. The ungodly struggle which was imposed on us was necessary. But we cannot rejoice in the success we have won over our brothers. Even after the victory we shall continue to wear mourning for those of us who fell in Syria, as well for those who fought in our ranks as our adversaries, victims of the treachery of a few men who have sacrificed France better to serve Hitler.' The gravestones of the dead on both sides bore only one inscription: 'Died for France'.

On 14th July, the armistice of Saint John of Acre, directly negotiated by Dentz and Wilson, put an end to the struggle. The problem of French sovereignty was passed over. It was a purely technical settlement which ignored 'the French who are traitors to their country like de Gaulle and Catroux.' In principle, it left Vichy entitled to consider itself as the mandatory power in the Lebanon and Syria and the French troops received the honours of war. Before being repatriated to France they were regrouped and their heavy armament was placed at the disposal of the British.

This settlement, though signed in the presence of General Catroux, aroused de Gaulle's anger. The British had played the Vichy game and had agreed to ignore the Free French. Catroux had fallen into the trap.

Finally, the terms of the armistice were an obstacle to winning over an important section of Dentz's army. According to Catroux, only 2,000 men in all joined the ranks of the Free French.

On 24th July, in Cairo, de Gaulle threatened to take full and complete control of the Free French forces in Syria and the Lebanon. After some tough talking, he persuaded Oliver Lyttelton, resident chargé d'affaires in the Middle East, to agree to an 'interpretative ordering' of the text of the armistice and an agreement on cooperation between the Free French and the British authorities in the Middle East. It recognized the 'particular obligations of the French, towards the territory of Lebanon and Syria'. Nevertheless, the predominance of the British command was recognized since it disposed of greater forces. This clause was later the root of serious Anglo-French friction.

In fact, the Syrian affair opened a new chapter of Anglo-French rivalry in the Middle East. For a start, de Gaulle no longer showed himself keen to give satisfaction to the Arab Nationalists and to grant effective independence. In September, General Catroux declared: 'The Syrian State now enjoys rights and prerogatives fitted for an independent and sovereign state. The only restrictions on these rights will be those imposed by the state of war.' This reservation was badly received by the Nationalists, particularly since direct administration remained the rule and the local authorities were only empowered to deal with matters of secondary importance.

Moreover, Great Britain, aware of the rise of nationalism, intended to play the card of Arab unity. She fell back on Lawrence's idea of an Arab kingdom, encompassing the whole 'fertile crescent' for the greater glory of the Hachemite dynasty. Churchill declared to the House of Commons: 'There is no question that France should retain the position in Syria that she occupied before the war ... The independence of Syria is an essential part of our policy.' In Damascus, General Spears made contact with the Nationalists, which earned him the title 'false brother'. In any case, he showed himself in favour of immediate elections.

This pretension caused a complete break between Spears and de Gaulle. In August 1942, the General made for Cairo where Churchill then was. It was Richard Casey, Lyttelton's successor, who braved the storm: 'Elections? Are you having them in Egypt? And do you not think that the British authorities in the Middle East have more urgent tasks than to play politics in countries administered by France? To defeat Rommel, for instance!' This unpleasant remark angered Churchill, for Rommel's victories in the desert were the latest in a long run of British disasters. He decided to leave Spears in Beirut and on 29th September forced a confrontation with de Gaulle, in the presence of Pleven and Eden.

'Why do you refuse to allow elec-elections in Syria and the Lebanon? Great Britain has obligations towards the Arabs to respect democracy.'

'Great Britain's obligations have nothing to do with us.'

'You are claiming the inter-Allied command of Syria and the Lebanon for a Frenchman. It is Great Britain who assumes the preponderant responsibilities in the region.'

'The de Gaulle-Lyttelton agreements lay down that the command of a sector will be exercised by the representative of the nation which has the largest number of forces there.'

'All the difficulties between us come from your excessive concern with prestige ... After all, are you France? Other parts of France could be called in the course of events to play a greater part today.'

'If I am not France, why are you discussing her world interests with

De Gaulle arrives in Cairo to discuss the fate of Syria after its surrender to the Allies

me?'

'I repeat that General de Gaulle is trying to improve his personal position by making difficulties for Great Britain.'

'If I had wanted to advance my career, I would have stayed in Vichy where I would have been Pétain's Chief of Staff.'

Relations between Great Britain and the Free French had sunk to their lowest ebb. The grievances were not limited to the Middle East. For months de Gaulle had been bitterly reproaching Churchill for having set up only a paper blockade in front of Djibouti and for having impeded the desertion of 10,000 men from Vichy.

Above all, at the time of the crisis of 29th September, the General was still smarting from the Madagascar affair. On 5th May 1942, a strong British expedition had attacked the base of Diego Suarez at the northern tip of the great island. The British were attempting to secure an excellent roadstead and a 200-metre dock while at the same time offering British public opinion a consolation prize for the depressing series of defeats suffered in the Indian Ocean since December 1941. Mindful of the lessons they had learned in Dakar and Syria, they did not inform General de Gaulle of the operation. 'I do not want Madagascar,' Churchill said to the Free French leader. 'We have no ulterior motives. We have decided rightly or wrongly, that we will meet with less resistance from the Vichy troops if we stand alone.' The blow to his pride from this 'intolerable attack on France's rights' was not softened when, on the eve of his row with Churchill, the British landed at Majunga, Moronvia and Tamatava.

By the end of the month, the whole island was under British control and de Gaulle's worst suspicions were confirmed. Even when, at the end of the year, the administration of Madagascar was handed back to the Free French, the General's bitterness remained.

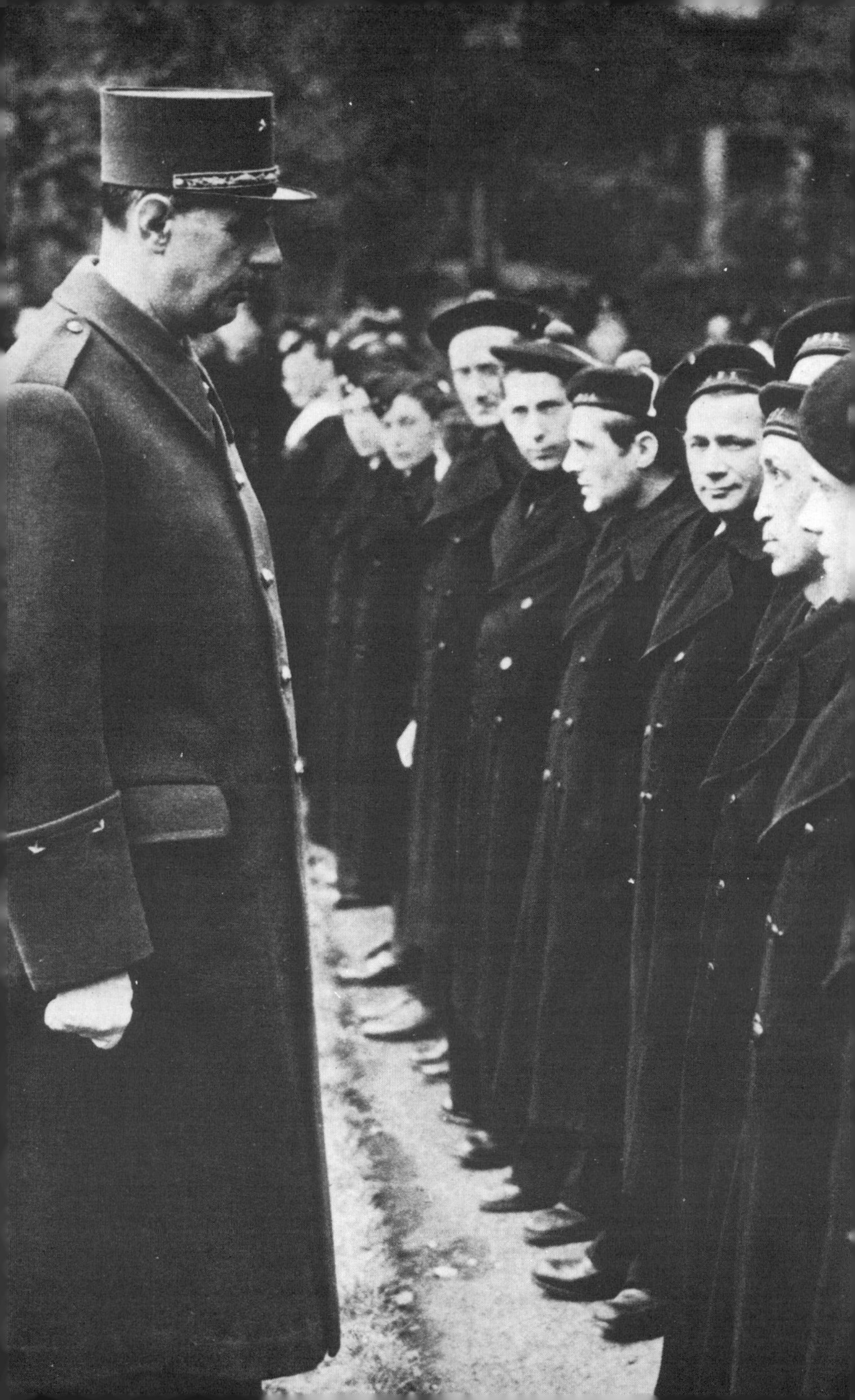

'Between East and West'

The relationship between the Free French and the Americans was worse, even, that with the British. Ever since 1940 relations between de Gaulle and Washington had been strained. The United States recognized the Vichy régime and their ambassador, Admiral Leahy, was a valuable prop for Pétain. Aware of the Marshal's popularity in the free zone and even in occupied France, the ambassador endeavoured to promote the delicate balancing act of the Vichy government and to ensure the rigorous application of the armistice.

In the United States the FreeFrench movement did not always have a good press. Here France's dirty linen was hung up for all to see. The Gaullist committee, 'France in spite of all', managed to win over a certain number of supporters and to obtain the backing of a section of the press. But it came up against the powerful Vichy propaganda machine and the undisguised hostility of certain influential personalities like Alexis Léger, Henri de Kérilis, and Camille Chautemps who, while repudiating the armistice and the Vichy régime, considered de Gaulle an 'apprentice dictator', in no way representative of French opinion. Finally, the Secretary of State for Foreign Affairs, Cordell Hull, instinctively mistrusted the General. As far as the State Department was concerned, the defeat at Dakar was mainly due to the rashness and bluster of the Free French.

But de Gaulle could not afford to ignore the United States. His aim was to obtain recognition of his movement, at least in practice. In the early summer of 1941, he decided to send an emissary of the Free French to Washington. The man chosen was René Pleven, who had strong connections in America. Convinced that the 'United States bring elementary feelings and complicated politics to bear on matters of worldwide importance,' he wanted to arrive at an agreement with Washington, but 'on a practical basis' and 'with our feet firmly on the ground'. As with Great Britain, he intended to enter into discussions 'as an equal' and on 'a reciprocal basis', however weak his position and his resources.

At first glance, the results seemed mediocre. Pleven succeeded in meeting the Under-Secretary of State, Summer Wells, only after great difficulty and his welcome was cold. America certainly intended to re-

De Gaulle inspects troops from Saint Pierre and Miquelon

Admiral Leahy, American ambassador to the Vichy government

establish French power, but there was disagreement as to the means. Nevertheless, a few faltering steps forward were made in the autumn. The State Department authorized the American Ambassador in London, Biddle, to keep in touch with the National Committee. The Free French would be able to benefit from the Lend-Lease law, but only through the intermediary of Great Britain. Cordell Hull made it clear that the United States would agree to give the Free French 'material aid whereever it is necessary, and would remain in contact with the Free French through its consular representative, but without recognizing them as a government.'

Washington intended to deal only with local representatives of the Free French. It was thus that the State Department agreed to a visit from a delegation headed by the syndicalist, Adrien Tixier. After Pearl Harbor, this delegation was empowered to undertake the problem of constructing an airfield for the US Air Force at Noumea in New Caledonia. At the moment when America found herself hurled into the war, Washington continued to recognize Vichy as the only legitimate authority.

De Gaulle's achievement of recognition of his National Committee was to a great extent swept away by a veritable tornado which cast a lasting shadow on the relations between the Free French and Washington. The first incident occurred when the United States was requisitioning French commercial ships anchored in American ports, in particular the liner *Normandie*. The decision to requisition the ship was taken without reference to the Free French delegation, nor for that matter to the Vichy government. De Gaulle did not hide his irritation, especially as he had the means of arming these vessels.

This incident was followed by the Saint-Pierre and Miquelon affair. For several months, the Americans and Canadians had been interested in a little archipelago which had remained loyal to Vichy and whose

Cordell Hull, American Secretary of State. Although America pledged material support to the Free French, the Vichy government was still recognised as the effective government of France

Alexis Léger. He, like many others who repudiated the Armistice and the Vichy regime, considered de Gaulle an 'apprentice dictator'

strategic position could not be missed at a time when the battle of the Atlantic was raging. The islands might serve as a fuelling base for the U-boats at any time and there was a powerful radio station. Finally, at the beginning of December 1941, at the Canadian government's request, Washington accepted that the radio station should be controlled by Canadian technicians.

But it was at this time, despite warnings from Britain, that de Gaulle decided to win over Saint-Pierre and Miquelon and even the Antilles, where the Americans had just reached a *modus vivendi* with Admiral Robert who still remained loyal to Vichy. For the leader of the Free French, the operation was a 'domestic affair' At the end of November, Admiral Muselier received the order to set sail from Scotland with the few Free French corvettes. Muselier was still reluctant to act without American or Canadian agreement and on 15th December in Ottawa he met Moffat, the Canadian Minister of foreign affairs. Moffat did not attempt to hide the reservations of the State Department and advised patience and prudence: Canadian control would only be temporary and sooner or later, Saint-Pierre and Miquelon would be returned to the Free French.

De Gaulle then decided to precipitate matters and to disregard American opposition. On 17th December he sent a threatening telegram to Admiral Muselier: 'We have, as you asked, consulted the British and American Governments. We know for certain that the Canadians intend to destroy the radio station at Saint-Pierre. In these circumstances, I order you to proceed with the takeover of Saint-Pierre and Miquelon with your own resources and to say nothing to the foreigners. I take entire responsibility for this operation, which is now indispensable if we are to retain for France her colonial possessions.'

Swallowing his reluctance, the Admiral went into action on 20th December 1941 and achieved his ob-

Camille Chautemps, former French Prime Minister and keen critic of de Gaulle

jective without the slightest opposition. A plebisicite sanctioned the operation. The inhabitants of Saint-Pierre were not asked to choose between de Gaulle and Pétain, but between the Free French and collaboration with the Axis powers.

Meanwhile, the Saint-Pierre and Miquelon operation, which took place concurrent with the Arcadia conference in which Roosevelt, Churchill and MacKenzie-King took part, raised an outcry of indignation from the State Department. The action of the 'so-called Free French' irritated Washington for two reasons: it had taken place at a critical moment in the Pacific War, and above all, it threatened to bring into question America's policy towards Vichy.

Cordell Hull did not mince words with Churchill: De Gaulle is a 'trouble monger' who is acting 'in flagrant contradiction to the desires of Great Britain, Canada and the United States'. So far, America had managed to see that the fleet and the French colonies escaped the grasp of the Germans. It was inadmissible that 'very great advantages should be rejected and thrown overboard to satisfy the whims of General de Gaulle and his band of followers'. As Admiral Leahy pointed out, the Germans could use the action of the Free French leader as a reason for pushing their troops into North Africa 'to safeguard it against a likely invasion'.

Embarrassed by the 'indiscretion' of their protégé, the British attempted to play down the affair and reduce it to its true proportions. Eden admitted to the United States Ambassador in London that 'the Free French had put themselves in the wrong and had committed an error, but he hoped that they [the United States] would consider

Burning at her berth in the port of New York, the French liner *Normandie*, requisitioned by the Americans and renamed the USS *Lafayette* without consulting either the Vichy government or the Free French

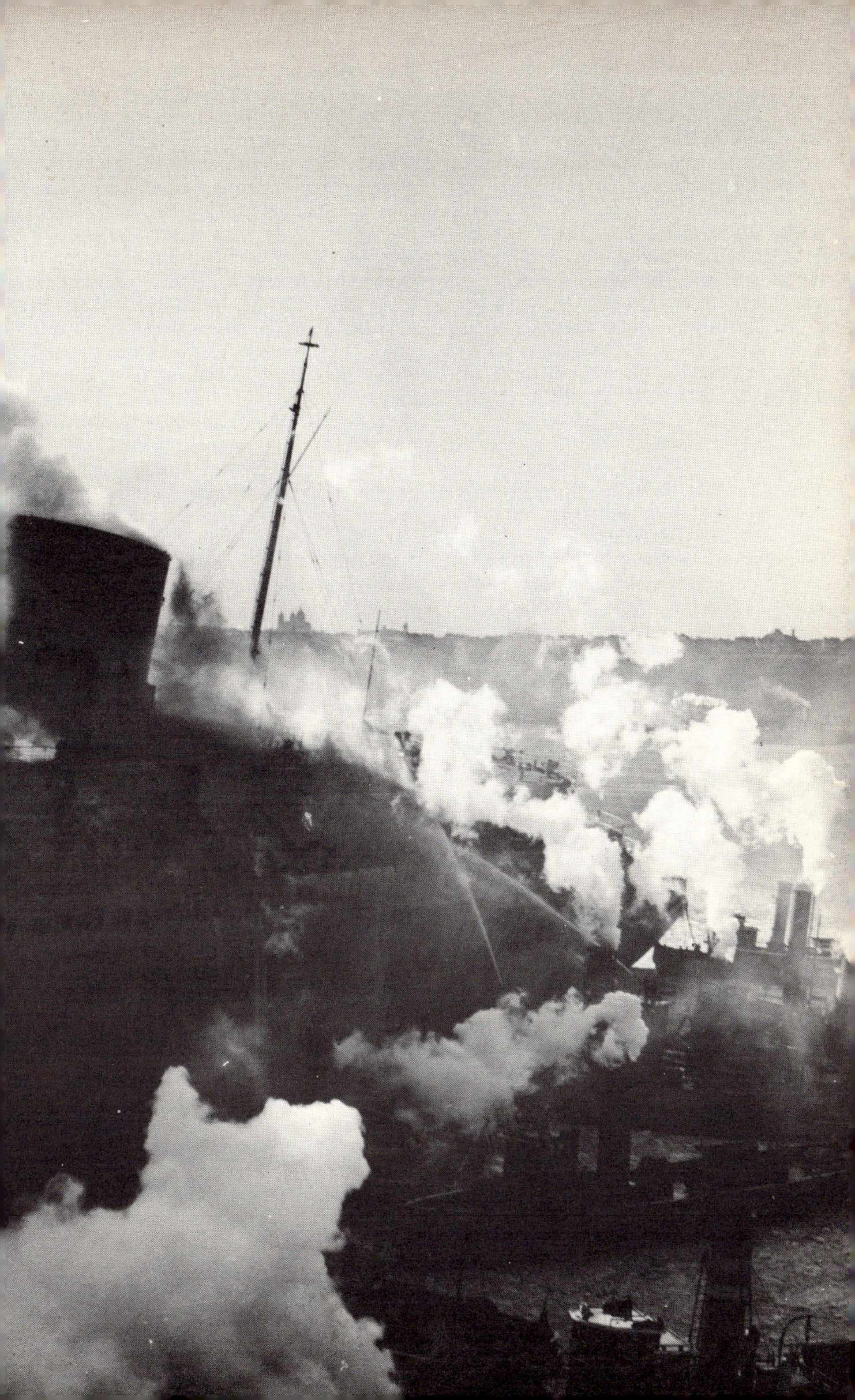

the incident in the light of the whole situation which had arisen from the war . . . In his opinion it would be as great a mistake to humiliate de Gaulle as to consolidate the Vichy government at that time.'

Finally, having considered a return to the *status quo*, if necessary by force, Cordell Hull finished by supporting the idea of an agreement 'which would allow the Free French to withdraw from the islands in a manner acceptable to de Gaulle'. Saint-Pierre and Miquelon would be neutralized, disarmed and administered by the three powers.

In the minds of most American officials, de Gaulle was either 'an instrument of British imperialism or just a political adventurer.' For Cordell Hull, 'de Gaulle has violated his obligations towards Great Britain, he is entirely responsible. He has also acted in formal contradiction to the desires of Canada and the United States. We considered him ambitious, concerned with his personal glory and less worthy of the trust we had accorded him until then.'

It was after the affair of Saint-Pierre and Miquelon that Roosevelt seems to have felt a 'morbid hostility' towards the Free French. According to his son, he said:'I cannot imagine a man for whom I could have greater distrust.' He considered him a creature of the English, 'jacket and tie included'. The British had provided him with 'the money, the equipment and the inspiration' necessary to set up his movement.

So the crisis of December 1941 was a turning point in the relations between the Free French and the Allies. Until that time, the attitude of the US towards de Gaulle had been largely dependent on its policy *vis-à-vis* Vichy. But after the Saint-Pierre and Miquelon crisis the Allies began to demonstrate a marked hostility towards him.

During the whole of 1942, relations between the Free French and Washington remained strained. The only positive point was an agreement that the Gaullist movement might benefit directly from the Lend-Lease law. Otherwise, the picture was bleak. De Gaulle was not informed of the Allies' strategic plans, nor of Operation Jubilee, the Dieppe raid. The Americans managed to convince the British of the necessity of keeping him out of Operation Torch and they started to look for a 'reliable interlocutor' in North Africa. Besides, Roosevelt felt that the French people, when they were finally liberated, should choose the form of government and the leaders which suited them. De Gaulle did not seem to be representative of French public opinion and recognition of the National Committee in France seemed more and more unlikely. The President's ideal would be to confine de Gaulle to a purely military role where he would have the chance to show his talents.

At the height of the tension with the Anglo-Saxons, de Gaulle sought an opening in the East. As soon as the German attack on the Soviet Union was announced, the General, who was then in Beirut, sent one of his representatives, Géraud Jouve, to Ankara to meet the Russian Ambassador, Vinogradov. The question of a permanent mission to Moscow was immediately considered, even if it did not mean official recognition of the Free French.

There are several reasons behind de Gaulle's approach to the USSR. He was motivated by a wish to perpetuate 'the policy of balance' already being played out between the East and West and he was concerned not to tie France down to any system of alliances. As early as 10th August 1941 Jouve stated: 'The General believes that France and Russia, who have maintained friendly relations for centuries,and who also realize what is necessary for Europe, could usefully collaborate once we are at peace . . . It is evident to him that the Anglo-Saxon bloc has other interests than those of Europe. General de Gaulle believes that the present war is a genuine revolution. For him, the question of political systems does not arise.'

Apart from this, de Gaulle believed that, given American neutrality, only the intervention of the USSR could bring the war out of its present impasse and secure the defeat of Germany. 'No one can say when victory will come,' said Jouve, 'but de Gaulle is now convinced that sooner or later the Germans will be crushed.' And there was another aspect he had to take into account. The Soviet Union's entry into the war had accentuated the ideological nature of the struggle. Barbarossa was the signal for French Communists to take part in the Resistance, to mount a massive campaign against the occupying forces. This phenomenon would necessarily modify the physionomy of France after the war. It was thus in her interest to promote good relations with Moscow.

Finally, the rapprochement with the USSR kindled in de Gaulle the hope that he might throw off the tutelage of Great Britain. On several occasions, both during Dejean's mission to Moscow in January 1942 and Molotov's visit to London in May of the same year, the General aired his grievances about the British and the Americans, who were trying 'to reduce the Free French to a purely military role, without political significance'.

In the short term, de Gaulle reaped very few advantages from his advances to Moscow. True, the Kremlin recognized the French National Committee from its formation in September 1941 and Bogomolov was accredited Ambassador to the Free French, as to all the governments-in-exile in London. A suggestion of military aid, with the posting of Free French troops to the Russian Front, came to nothing because of British objections. In the end, only airmen of the Normandy-Niemen squadron were sent. The most curious aspect of the relationship between de Gaulle and Moscow lay elsewhere. According to Soviet documents published in 1959 – the de Gaulle Memoirs

Maisky, the Soviet ambassador in London. He denounced de Gaulle's 'fascist' tendencies and characterised him as the modern Napoleon

breathe not a word about it – de Gaulle had considered breaking with London in 1942 and transferring his organization to Russia. At that time he suspected the Americans of having designs on Dakar and the British of wanting to annexe Nigeria, without the assistance of the Free French. Ten days later, the Gerneral decided to abandon his plan because of assurances given by the Anglo-Saxons.

In reality, the Russians, too, were circumspect in their dealings with de Gaulle. A report from Maisky dated January 1942 denounced his 'fascist' tendencies, characterized him as a modern Napoleon, and criticized his politics.

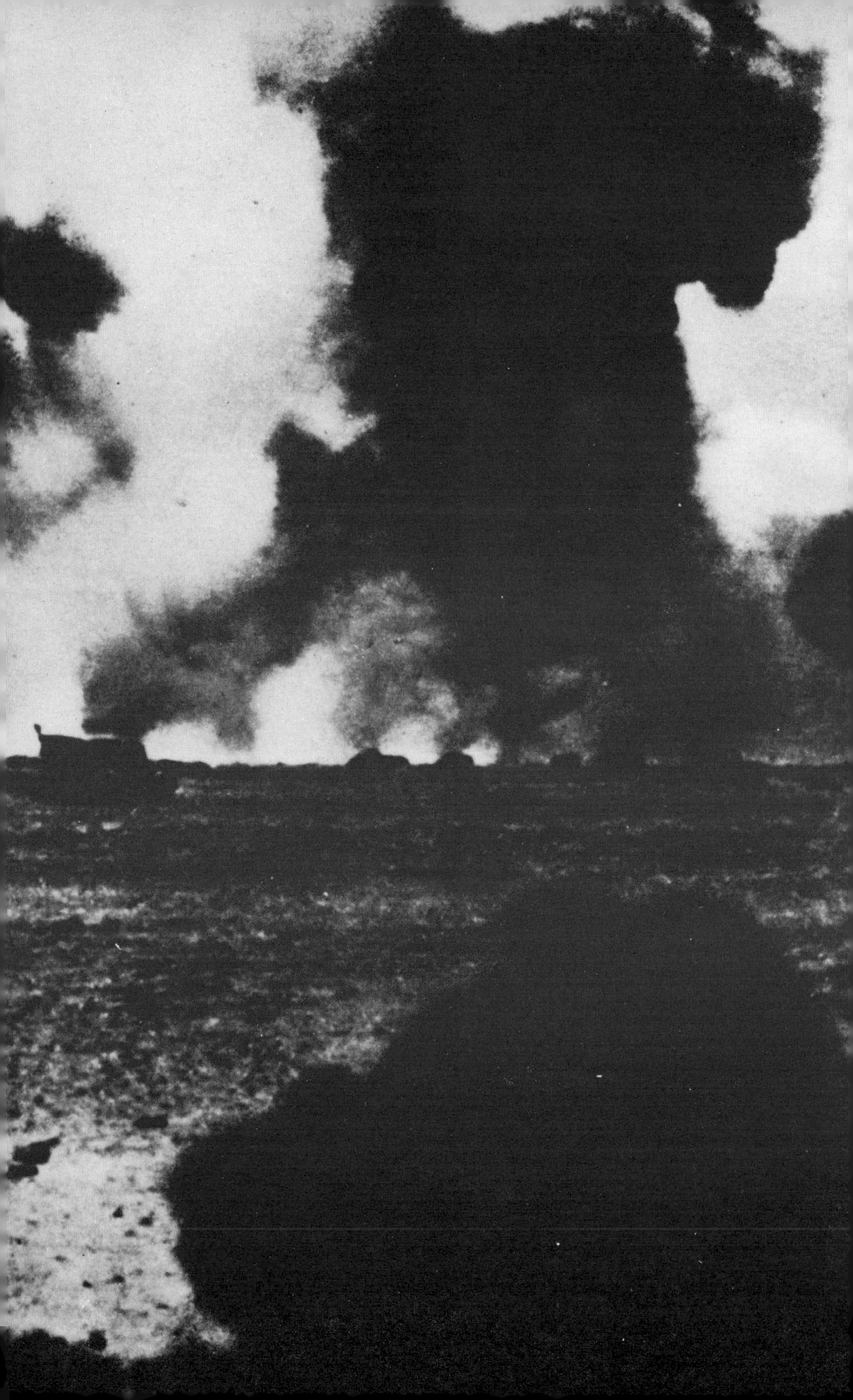

North Africa

At the end of 1942, with the outcome of the war being decided at Stalingrad and El Alamein, the situation of the Gaullist movement remained precarious. In order to 'help the Free French to claim the rights that are denied to them', de Gaulle was counting on the courage and self sacrifice of those who had answered his call. The movement was now nearly 70,000 strong, but only 20,000 men could be counted as fighting troops. Nevertheless, the General intended his forces, however small, to take part in the struggle in as many different theatres as possible.

The small Free French Naval Force was above all the creation of Admiral Muselier, replaced by Admiral Auboyneau in 1942. From the end of 1940, a few hundred volunteers had managed to re-arm several despatch-boats, three destroyers and several submarines, all of which were of French construction. This was the heroic period of the Free French Naval Forces. From 1942 there the British agreed to provide the French with half a dozen corvettes which took part in the interminable and merciless Battle of the Atlantic. It was thus that the *Alysse* and the

Bir Hakeim under attack. Koenig's men gave an excellent account of themselves and repaired their reputation

Mimosa were torpedoed in December 1941 and June 1942. But the *Aconit* achieved the success of sinking two submarines in twenty-four hours.

It was on land that the Free French, now the Fighting French, carried out their most famous exploits. In 1941, the 'Monclar brigade' from Douala, consisting of two battalions of the Foreign Legion, joined the British in the conquest of Eritrea and the capture of Massaoua. Greatly reinforced, the brigade, now the 1st Free French Division, won renown in Libya in 1942 at Bir Hakeim. General Koenig's 3,400 men occupied a key position to the south of the British forces. Subjected to attack after attack by Italian tanks, then by German guns, and finally by the Luftwaffe, they held out from 26th May until 10th June. A daring breakout finally permitted two-thirds of the little garrison to rejoin the British.

With the passing of time, the 'victory' of Bir Hakeim has taken on the character of a legend in the annals of French military history. It has almost been forgotten that Koenig's brave little band played just one part in a battle involving several hundreds of thousands of men, and which ended in one of the greatest Allied defeats of the war, followed by the loss of Tobruk.

Above: Admiral Auboyneau, successor to Muselier as chief of Free French naval forces. *Below:* General Koenig, commander of the Free French forces at Bir Hakeim, Libya, 1942. *Right:* De Gaulle and Leclerc in the spring of 1941

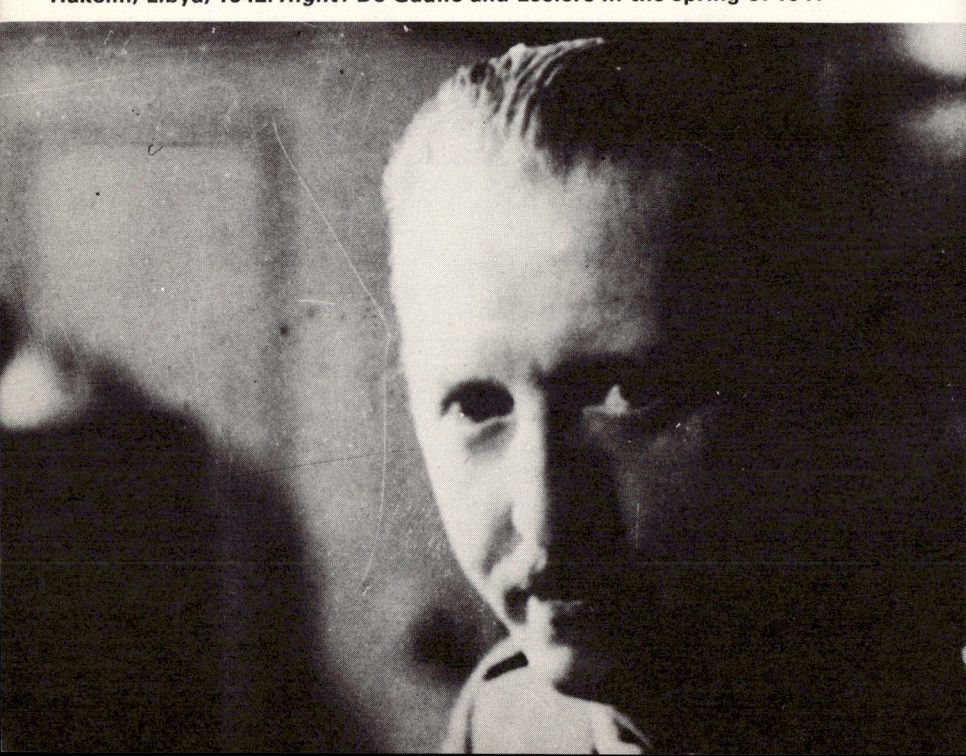

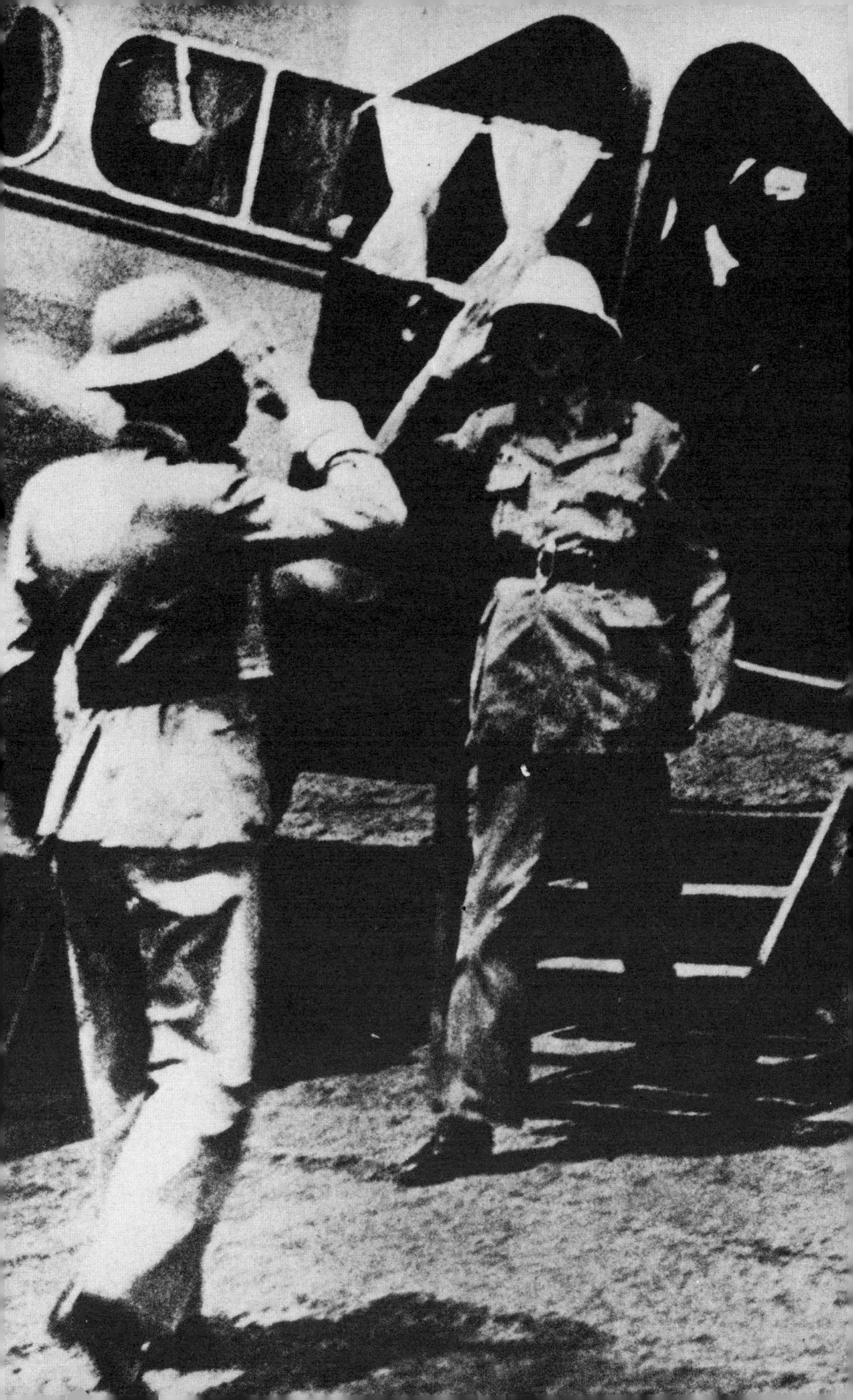

But the episode of Bir Hakeim nevertheless contributed towards the rehabilitation of the French army. The garrison had held out for fourteen days instead of the expected two and Rommel wrote: 'It is proof that a leader who has decided not to throw down his rifle at the first opportunity can achieve miracles.'

By this time, Leclerc had already laid the foundations of the future 2nd Armoured Division. As early as the autumn of 1940, in the course of his visit to Africa, de Gaulle had declared his intention of 'opening a front in the Sahara'. His aim was twofold: to commit his forces in the struggle at once and, while awaiting a final settlement, to take an option on the oasis of Italian Fezzan. Leclerc was given the task and promoted to colonel for the purpose. In January 1941 he left Chad and, after a difficult march, managed to take the Italian post of Koufra. This was on 2nd March and it was there that Leclerc made his famous pledge to 'carry on the struggle until the French flag flies over Metz and over Strasbourg.' The following year, Leclerc led a harassing raid on Fezzan. But it was only at the end of 1942, after the victory of Alamein, that he decided to attempt a decisive expedition. The 'Leclerc column' comprised about 3,300 men at that time (of which only 550 were Europeans) and 350 vehicles. By mid-January 1943, they had occupied the oases of Fezzan and on 26th January, having covered several hundred miles and posing a real threat to the right flank of Rommel's army-then in full retreat, they reached Tripoli where they received an enthusiastic welcome from the 1st Free French Division. Then, attached to the Eighth Army, Leclerc took part in the pursuit of Afrika Korps, reaching southern Tunisia in February.

Here for the first time Gaullists and Vichyites met, three months after the Allied landing in North Africa. 'We were expecting to rediscover each other,' said General Beaufre, 'but we were brought down to earth with a bump: there were accounts to be settled...' After more than two years of exile and doubt, the Free French Forces had assimilated their leader's hatred of Vichy. Condemned in their absence to death or to long terms of imprisonment, often deprived of their property by tribunals in their own country, they experienced all the bitterness of outcasts, of victims of an unjustifiable excommunication. They felt no inclination to fraternize with those who had taken up arms again just when victory was changing camps. On the day of the victory in Tunis the Gaullists refused to march alongside the troops of the Army of Africa.

On the night of 7th November 1942 Operation Torch began. It was inspired by the British but carried out almost entirely by the Americans. The Allied troops landed at several points on the coasts of Morocco and Algeria, at times meeting with fierce resistance. This operation, one of the turning points of the war, gave rise to the gravest crisis de Gaulle had faced since the Call of 18th June.

There is no need to expound the rather confused history behind Operation Torch. It is necessary simply to recall that the Americans, through their consul, Murphy, had 'come to understandings' with certain resistance groups on the spot, notably The Group of Five – Lemaigre-Dubreuil, Saint Hardouin, Jean Rigault, Van Eck, and Henri d'Astier de la Vigerie. On their side the conspirators assured themselves of the help of General Mast, commanding the Algiers division, and of General Bethouard commanding the Casablanca division. But it was General Giraud who, in principle, should have led the movement. His already considerable reputation in the army had been strengthened by his spectacular escape from the fortress of Koenigstein. For the Americans he constituted a 'reliable interlocutor'.

But things did not work out at all as expected. When Giraud, who had been

The 'Leclerc column' in Nigeria, 1943

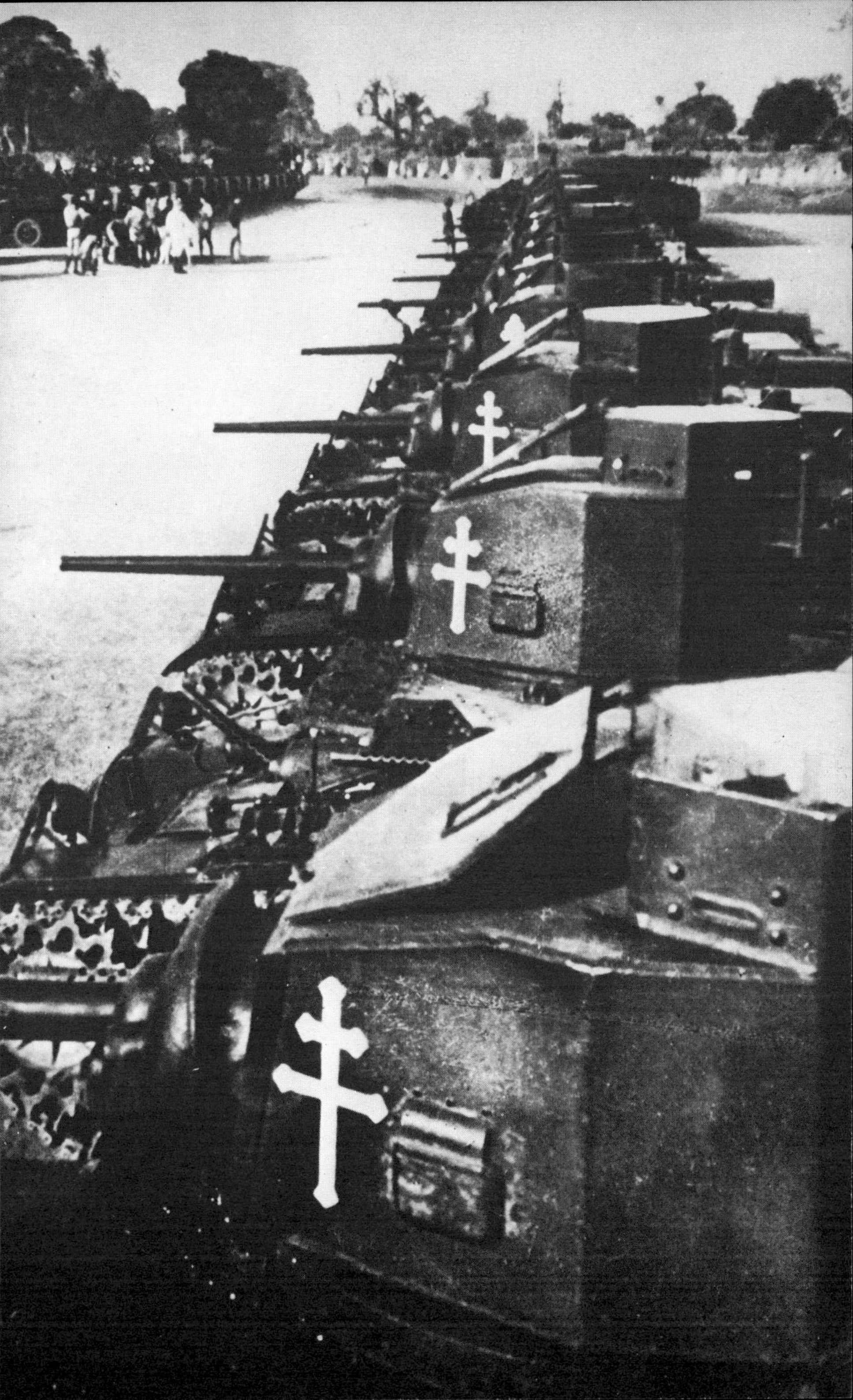

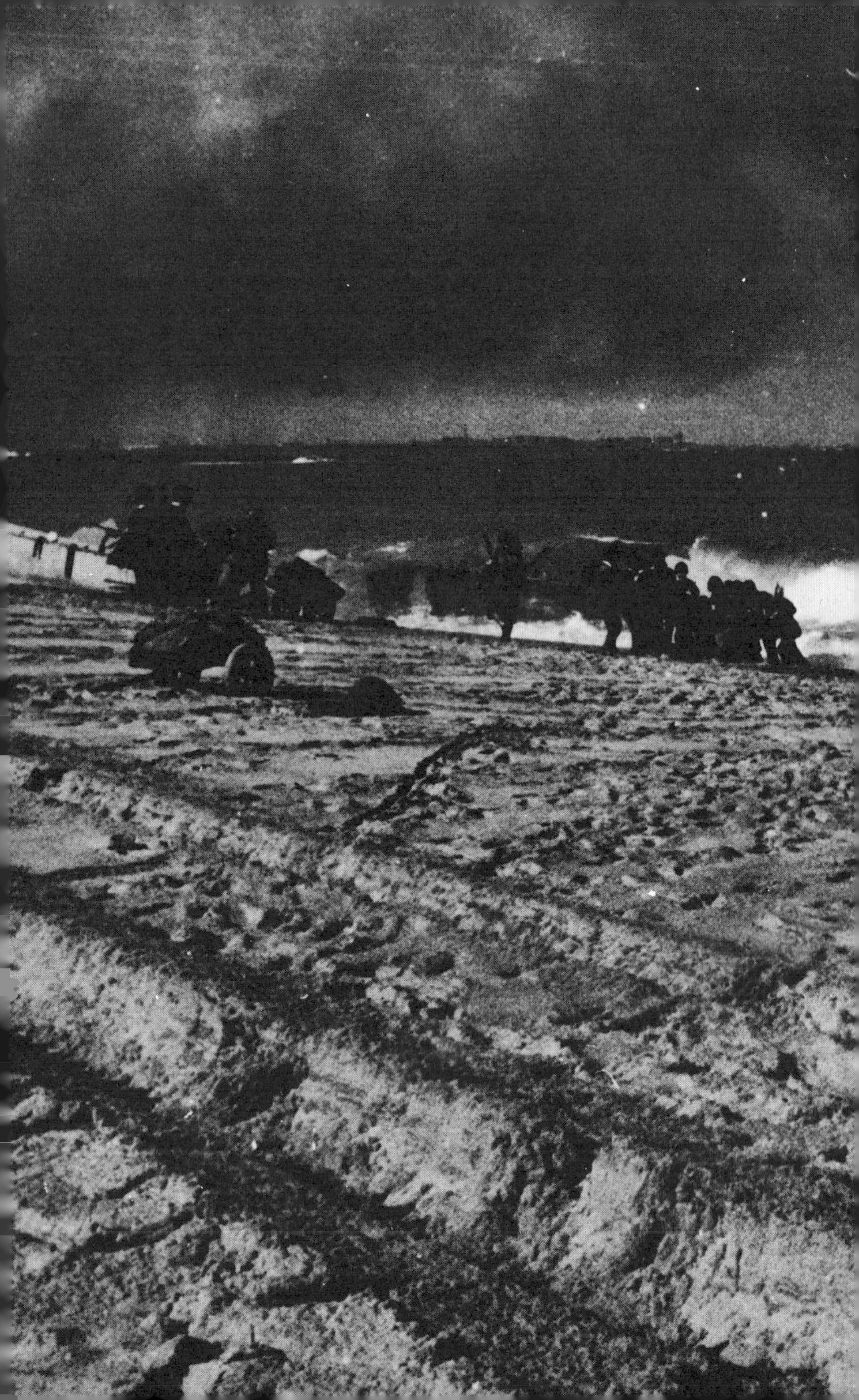

Operation Torch – American troops land in Morocco

held up in Gibraltar, landed in Algeria on 9th November, there was no one awaiting him. The strike launched on the night of the 7th had stalled and the commander of the American troops, General Clark, decided to play the Darlan card, as a 'temporary expedient'. The admiral, who happened to be in Algeria because his son was ill there, wielded great authority by virtue of his position as Minister of Defence and Admiral of the Fleet. It was thanks to him that a cease-fire was obtained in Algiers on the evening of the 8th. Two days later he received an ultra-secret message from Marshal Pétain: 'Do your best; I entrust you with the interests of the Empire.' Secure in Pétain's confidence, Darlan decided to sign an armistice with Clark, valid for the whole of North Africa. The fighting stopped immediately.

By the 13th the imbroglio seemed to have been resolved. General Eisenhower was Commander-in-Chief, but Admiral Darlan retained the upper hand in civil administration. With the title of High Commissioner, he was the real head of government. As for Giraud, who was only interested in returning to the struggle against the Boche, he was given command of land and air forces, while Darlan retained control of the fleet. A few days later, the Admiral set up his government, offering several posts to the 'Five'. Saint Hardouin took on Foreign Affairs, Rigault, assisted by Henri d'Astier de la Vigerie, the Interior. Finally, the Admiral set up an 'Empire Council' headed by himself, to which he appointed Bergeret, Giraud, Noguès, Chatel, the governor general of Algeria, and Boisson who had been won over on 23rd November.

These arrangements seemed to satisfy the greatest number. Authority was still exercised in the name of Vichy, which avoided any problems of conscience for the civil servants and the army who had sworn allegiance to the Marshal. The Crémieux decree remained abolished and Algerian Jews were still barred from French citizenship. As for the Americans, they were unencumbered by the problems of civil administration and they could concentrate on the Tunisian campaign with the help of the French African troops. The hesitation of Admiral Esteva and General Barre had allowed the Germans to install themselves in Tunis and Bizerta and to establish a liaison with Rommel's troops who were in full retreat across Libya. Roosevelt appeared satisfied and sent the following cable to Eisenhower: 'I realise that if Darlan and Co are of real service during the operations, it will have to be taken into account.'

The only people to show disappointment and anger were the partisans of the Comte de Paris, the monarchist pretender, and above all the Free French. De Gaulle did not hide his rage that he had not been warned. Angrily he declared to his aide de camp: 'I hope the Vichyites will kick them into the sea! You can't get into France by breaking and entering!' Nevertheless he agreed, the next day, to broadcast a hopeful message: 'Now the great moment has arrived! Now is the time for common sense and courage . . . Frenchmen of North Africa, through you we are coming back into line from one end of the Mediterranean to the other and now the war is won thanks to France.'

But he could not bring himself to accept the birth of another source of resistance, a rival to his own. He regarded the new recruits as workers of the eleventh hour. On 11th November, at the Albert Hall, de Gaulle delivered a warning: 'The centre round which unity is being forged again is us, the France which fights. To the imprisoned nation we have offered, ever since the first day, struggle and light . . . Let us not admit that whoever comes to divide the country's war effort by any of their so-called parallel enterprises . . . Is it not in the name of France that the French National Committee speaks?'

It was a new declaration of war, or

De Gaulle and General Giraud, C-in-C French forces in North Africa, meet in May 1943

rather the beginning of a new phase in the struggle against Vichy, more implacable than the first. But de Gaulle would have to play a cautious game. The whole existence of Fighting France was at stake.

The North African affair was not alone in bringing drawbacks. For a start, Operation Torch put an end to the Vichy mortgage. The old Marshal, despite pressing invitations, refused to go to Algiers, which might have dealt a fatal blow to the Gaullist movement. 'A pilot,' he said, 'should remain at the helm during the storm . . . if I had left, it would have meant that the fate of Poland would have become France's fate as well . . . it would have killed France.' In fact, the Marshal, long since 'adrift', was now simply an old man, albeit a great one, who, stubborn and vacillating, could not retain his lucidity for more than a few hours a day.

On 11th November, the Germans invaded the free zone. On the 27th, the French fleet was scuttled at Toulouse. Along with the Empire went the last hopes of a régime which no longer retained even the appearance of independence. Only the Vatican and Switzerland continued to keep a diplomatic representative at Vichy. Laval vainly persisted with a policy of collaboration that he realised was condemned by the majority of the country.

'What do you expect of me?' he asked pitifully, 'I am playing my hand on the assumption that the Germans will win the war. Are they going to win it? I do not know . . . as time goes by I think it less likely . . . There are two men who can help their country, General de Gaulle and myself. If the Germans win the war, perhaps I will be able to discuss an honourable peace treaty with them. If the Germans are beaten, General de Gaulle will return. He has behind him – I have no illusions on this score – 80 to 90 per cent of the population, As for me, I will be hanged . . . What difference does it make? If I was not Laval, I would want to be General de Gaulle.'

The French cruiser *Dupleix* lists and sinks as the French fleet is scuttled at Toulon, 27th November 1942

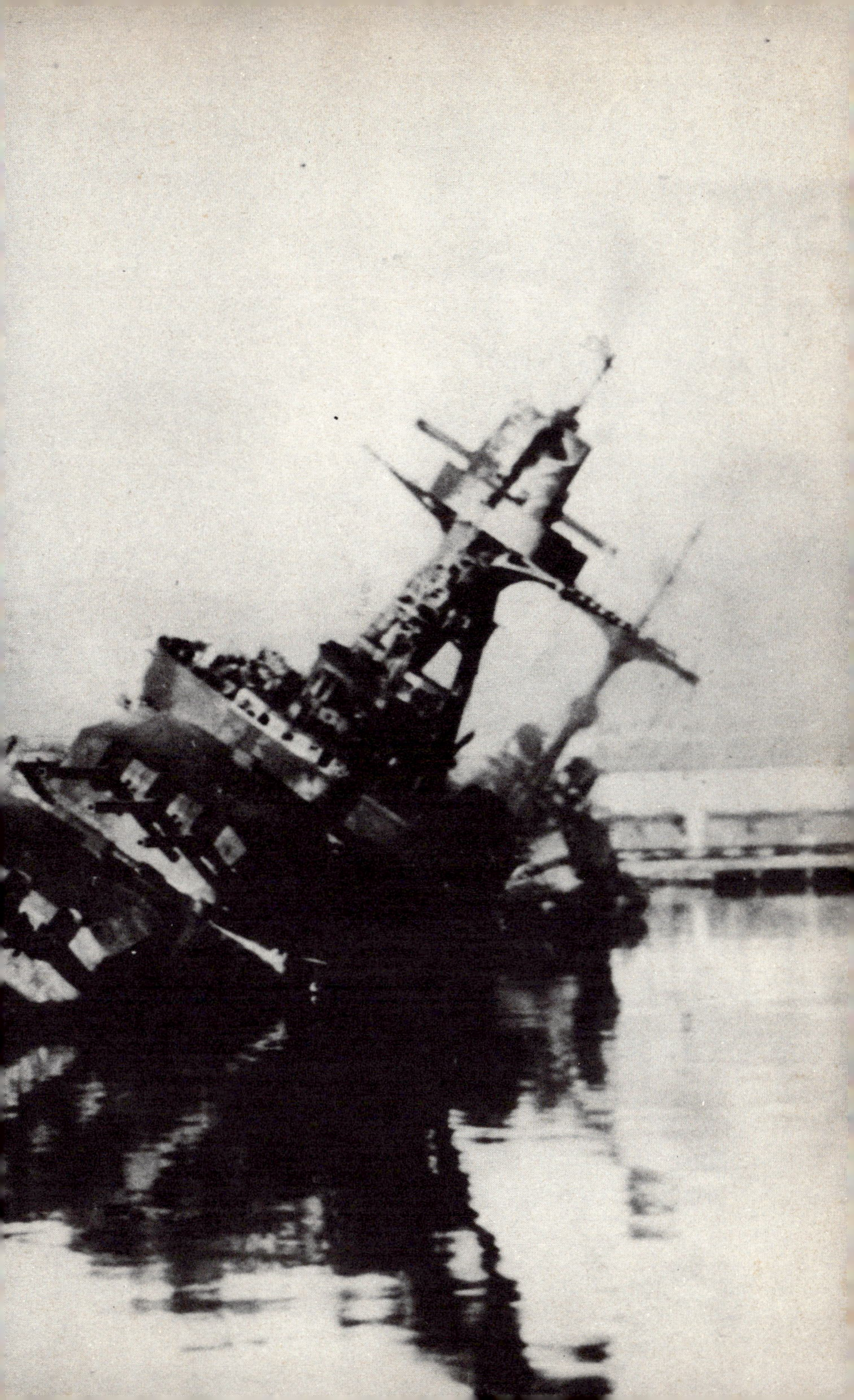

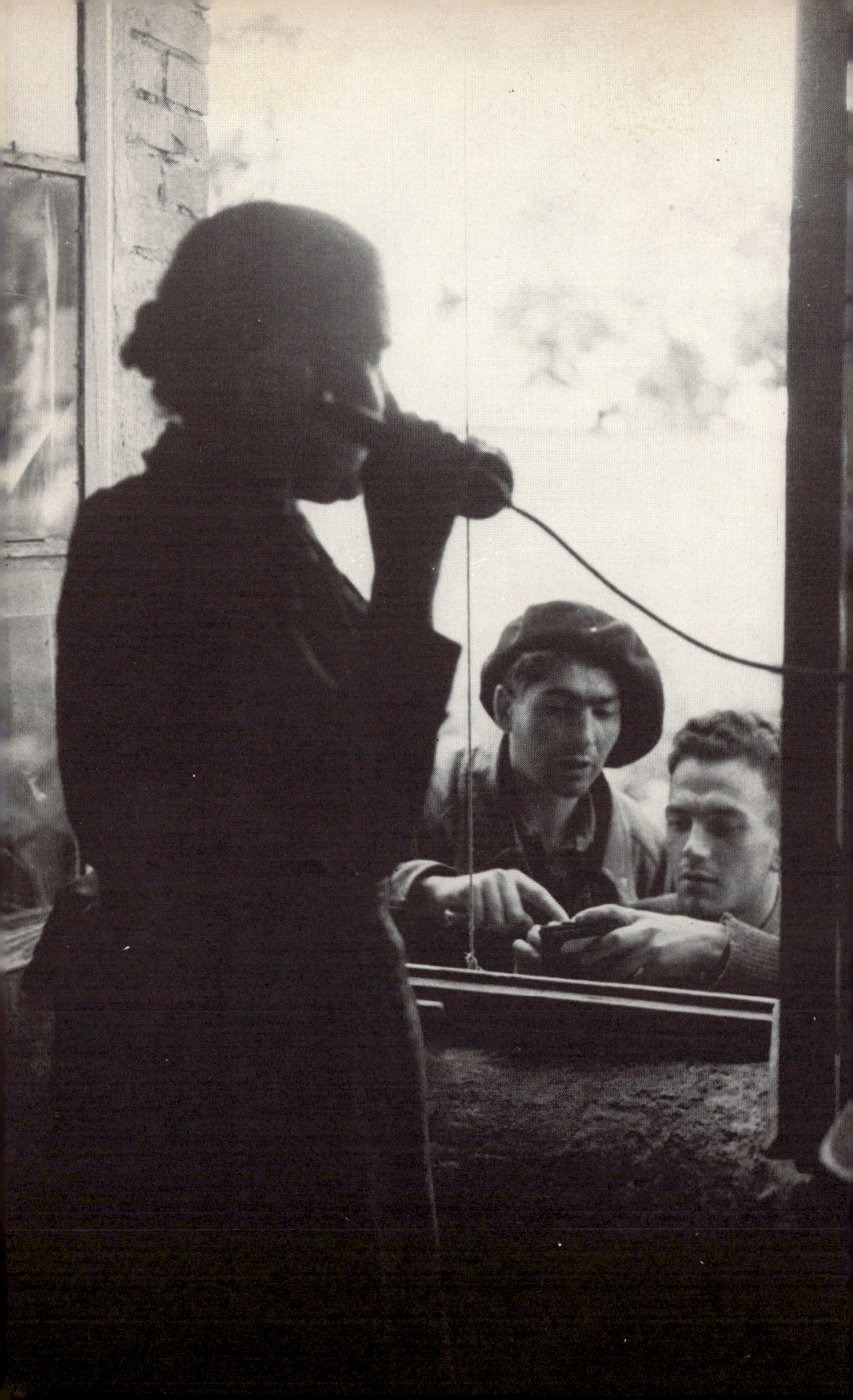

The Maquis

From 1943, the occupation became more and more a burden on the people of France, with the requisition of manpower and the growing shortage of provisions. For the French, there was no safety except abroad, even if the old Marshal continued to be the object of sentimental affection.

There remained the Darlan obstacle. With the man of Berchtesgaden no compromise was possible. It was the same with the 'proconsuls' who had taken the easy way, the 'path of dishonour' in June 1940. On 16th November, de Gaulle thundered on Brazzaville radio: 'The nation is asking itself, whether or not . . . the Liberation, starting from the liberated Empire, should be dishonoured by a handful of guilty men camouflaged, for the occasion, under an additional perjury.' There was no question of tolerating the survival of Vichy in Algiers in a disguised form, with or without the blessing of the Americans.

The General declared to Churchill: 'It is a strategic mistake to kick against the moral nature of this war. We are waging war today with our souls, our blood and the suffering of our people . . . If France were one day to acknowledge that, because of the Anglo-Saxons, her liberator was Darlan, you could perhaps win the war from a military point of view, but morally you would be the losers and indeed, there would be only one winner: Stalin.'

But Providence took a hand in events and the obstacle was removed. On 24th December, the Admiral was assassinated by a twenty-year old monarchist, Bonnier de la Chapelle. The murderer was tried the next day, condemned to death, and executed on the 26th. The speed with which the trial took place drew a curtain of obscurity over an already dark affair. It seems, however, that the assassination was perpetrated by a group of monarchist and Gaullist hot-heads who had decided to replace the Darlan solution with a formula which included the Comte de Paris, Giraud and de Gaulle. The Comte de Paris would have taken on the role of a lieutenant general, assisted by Giraud as military Commander-in-Chief and de Gaulle would have been responsible for civil affairs. There is nothing to prove that either the Comte de Paris or de Gaulle had a hand in the assassination, but the leader of the Free French never spoke of the 'assassination' of Darlan, but rather of his 'execution'. The affair dragged on for some time.

Maquis liaise by telephone

Admiral Darlan, assassinated 24th December 1942

The Defence Council of the Empire met on the 26th and unanimously appointed Giraud as Darlan's successor, with the somewhat bizarre title of 'Military and Civilian Commander-in-Chief'.

In any event, Darlan's disappearance was of immense advantage to de Gaulle. Giraud did not suffer from any moral stigma and on 25th December de Gaulle permitted himself the luxury of offering the brave soldier a rapprochement and even a union of the only two movements which made up the French Resistance. Giraud did not reply until the 29th. He did not trust de Gaulle and the Gaullists. There were rumours in Algiers of a new attempt on his person and during the inquest on Darlan's assassination he had certain members of the Gaullist movement arrested... But there was to be no legal follow-up to the affair.

The first meeting between de Gaulle and Giraud came about under the auspices of the Allies. In mid-January 1943, at Anfa in the suburbs of Casablanca, a summit conference took place between Roosevelt, Churchill and the most important military leaders including Stalin. Giraud, who was cordially invited to attend, arrived on the 17th and had several discussions with Roosevelt and Churchill. As for de Gaulle, he was unwilling to reply to an invitation from 'foreigners' to visit 'sovereign French territory'. He decided to leave London only on the 22nd after he had been given an ultimatum from Churchill who was determined not to have a confrontation with the Americans on the subject of Fighting France. 'As soon as he arrived', Churchill noted, 'I had an icy discussion with him and I made it quite plain to him that we would not hesitate to break with him if he persisted in standing in our way. He appeared very stiff, then went out of the villa and crossed the garden with his head held very high.' A few days earlier Churchill had sent a telegram to Eden: 'If de Gaulle does not take the chance we are offering him today, I think that his replacement as leader of the Free French will become an essential condition to the continuation of the support given by His Majesty's Government.'

The interview with Giraud in the presence of Roosevelt and Churchill failed to achieve anything, other than a 'historic' handshake between the two men under the complacent camera eye of the Allied reporters. De Gaulle forced a smile, but it was obvious that his heart was not in the meeting. The opposition between the two men seemed to be irreconcilable. The leader of Fighting France refused the proposed solution: a Directory of Three, headed by Giraud in which he would play a secondary role with General Georges, whom the British special services were preparing to bring to France. In fact, de Gaulle intended to retain political leadership and to assign Giraud to purely military functions. 'You can be Foch and I will be Clémenceau...' he declared.

The rift between the two men seemed deep and difficult to heal. Giraud was a military man at heart and he could not rid himself of his respect for hierarchy. For him, the leader of the Free French remained 'petit de Gaulle', the mere colonel who was still under his command. The ratio of forces was in Giraud's favour. Two and a half years after the Call of 18th June, de Gaulle still had only one clearly defined territorial base, an often uncertain relationship with Syria and the Lebanon, Equitorial Africa and a smattering of territories in the Pacific. He had fewer than 100,000 men of whom only 20,000 were fighting troops. Giraud, on the other hand, headed a cohesive territorial group: the whole of North Africa except Tunisia, French West Africa, and soon the Antilles. His military forces comprised more than 300,000 men, not counting a fleet of nearly 300,000 tons with fine modern ships and several hundred trained pilots. Finally, the agreements made with the Americans led him to expect rearmament with modern materials in a short time. France would have a dozen divisions at her disposal.

Politically, there was a collision of two ideals. Giraud was unwilling to prejudice any political decisions that the French might take one peace had returned and the national territory was completely liberated. It was only then that the shape of a new régime would become clear. In the meantime he believed that the main problem was to continue the struggle on the side of the Allies and in the framework of their strategy. France had to rehabili-

General Giraud, President Roosevelt, General de Gaulle and Winston Churchill at the Casablanca conference January 1943. De Gaulle forces a smile for the handshake with Giraud

tate herself on the field of battle as she had already done in Tunisia. After the war, her place in the world, her prestige, her authority would ultimately depend on the importance and the quality of her participation in it.

For the time being, Giraud proposed the creation of an Administrative Council composed of the governors and residents of the colonial territories. De Gaulle could take part in the capacity of vice-president. After the liberation of France, the councillors could, by virtue of the law of Treveneuc of 1872, appoint a provisional government. Giraud had no intention of authorizing the reconstitution of a communist party which had fallen into discredit since the Nazi-Soviet Pact of 1939 and which took its cue from abroad. Furthermore, the ex-governor of Metz intended to restore the union of all the French, whatever their roles during France's dishonour, with the obvious exception of traitors and proven collaborators. He intended to retain the men nominated by Vichy in the army and the administration and to respect the institutional framework established by the Marshal.

De Gaulle's ideas conflicted strongly with this programme. He rejected the idea of an Administrative Council. If France were to give herself a provisional government, it must be nothing but an enlarged Defence Committee, responsible for all France's interests and able to negotiate with the Allies on an equal footing. What de Gaulle disliked in Giraud was that he put himself 'at the discretion of the Americans. He is mortgaging himself to America,' he declared to Bonscat 'He is laying the foundations of France's servitude and courting serious disillusion.' He could not forgive Giraud for having taken upon himself, as French Commander-in-Chief in Algiers, 'the right and duty of upholding all the interests of France, military, financial, economic and moral.' Until the day when the French people and nation could appoint their own government, the Allies had no right to intervene in purely French affairs. Similarly, he would not countenance a rate of exchange he judged unfavourable. De Gaulle still envisaged a provisional consultative assembly which would bring together delegates of the resistance movements and the parties which had not tainted themselves with Vichy. Finally, he believed that the functions of a Commander-in-Chief were incompatible with those of a member of a government.

All these ideas appear in a memorandum of 23rd February 1943. There was only one way out for the Algerians: to submit and to identify themselves with the Defence Committee. 'Giraud represents nothing', affirmed de Gaulle. 'All I can do is to invite him to sit at a table with me. Nothing more!' Finally de Gaulle dismissed the idea of a reconciliation. The General's hostility towards Vichy and that of most of his entourage bordered on hatred. At the time of the Saint-Pierre and Miquelon affair, de Gaulle is supposed to have said to General Odic who had just left to join the Free French: 'The Marshal is a traitor and I will have him shot. General Weygand is a traitor and I will have him shot. I will do the same to the others.' To Colonel Solberg who was singing the praises of certain 'fine Frenchmen' like Boisson and Noguès, the General replied: 'There are no fine Frenchmen who have not followed me.' He intended eventually to execute most of the civilian and military leaders appointed by Vichy, starting with the colonial governors: 'Giraud is a prisoner of the great feudal lords of Vichy who bestow honours upon him and use him as an honourable façade.' As for the Army of Africa, he did not hide from General Bouscat his belief 'that it must be purged, maybe even dissolved. In any case one must take steps to ensure that a new army will be created.'

By the end of February 1943, agreement seemed further away than ever. It looked as though the resistance outside France might split into two factions: one in Algiers, patronized by the Americans, and one in London, relying on the increasingly 'conditional' support of Churchill. But for several reasons the situation changed.

It was clear that de Gaulle had the advantage over his adversary in ingenuity and political experience. Giraud was above all a soldier, a 'fighter', with a magnificent record of service in Morocco. But if his performance as an army commander in 1940 was anything to go by, the conclusions to be drawn from his behaviour were not all favourable. He seemed to manifest a certain 'allergy' to modern warfare. His idea of an American landing in the South of France in November 1942 betrayed a disturbing lack of perception and a profound misunderstanding of the plain facts of logistics. Equally, his plan for taking the whole German military machine in Western Europe 'in the rear' with the sole help of the armistice army whose armour was limited to a few dozen tanks was perplexing. General Beaufre, while agreeing that he had certain admirable qualities, had to admit that he had a simplistic mind.

For all his fine presence and his magnificent moustache, Giraud was a man of disarming naiveté and completely unsuited to the rough and tumble of politics. In November 1942 in Gibraltar, he fondly imagined that he would obtain the command of *all* the Allied forces the day after the landing in North Africa. But one must not forget that he was responsible for the reorganization of the French troops in North Africa and that he gave valuable advice to Eisenhower in Tunisia. It was thanks to him that France had a modern army at her disposal in 1944, an army which fought valiantly in Italy, in Provence and in Alsace. Certainly de Gaulle would never have been able to obtain such important material assistance from the Americans with Giraud's efforts – and it was this which helped restore France's prestige.

But the struggle between the two men was an unequal one. In two and a half years de Gaulle had acquired formidable experience and he now proved himself a remarkable tactician in politics, sure of himself and of the moral values he represented. General Bouscat was aware of this as soon as he arrived in London. 'I had before me a man obviously trained for the exercise of power; he was a man who had acquired great self-confidence. He had succeeded in an important task, both dangerous and difficult. This success was his own achievement and his alone, a monument to his intelligence, his will, and his energy. He is totally convinced of his talent and this assurance dominates his personality. The inevitable result? He is ambitious, very ambitious. And I come away sharing his own absolute certainty that France awaits him, that the French people want him and want only him.'

De Gaulle succeeded first in strengthening his position on the very home ground of his rival. In Algiers, the little group of Gaullists led by René Capitant, who ran the newspaper *Combat*, indulged in a frenetic attempt

René Capitant, leader of the Gaullists in Algiers who tried to discredit Giraud

A pamphlet issued by the National Union of Journalists to commemorate clandestine newspapers printed in occupied and freed zones

to discredit Giraud, whom they represented as the arch-reactionary general. The Gaullists also had the support of the Jews, who were still subject to Vichy legislation and deprived of civil rights, and of the communists, who laboured under the ban imposed on their party in 1939. A certain number of them had been freed from prison, but they were forbidden to take part in any political activity. Finally, the Gaullists launched a full-scale enticement campaign among the North African troops and the naval and air forces in Algiers. The results were not spectacular; only 2,000 men were won over. The campaign provoked serious friction and even difficulties abroad. In New York, the Americans felt obliged to isolate the battleship *Richelieu* in an effort to call a halt to the 'desertions'.

But de Gaulle achieved a masterstroke in putting himself forward as coordinator and representative of the home resistance movements struggling against Vichy and the occupation. The Call of 18th June had contained no incitement to an armed struggle against the Germans and the champion of the armoured weapon seemed to have given little thought to subversive warfare prior to 1940.

The first contact between London and the home resistance movement was made at the end of 1940. At that time a certain number of officers and intellectuals had set up movements which refused to accept defeat and which had disputed the authority of the Vichy régime. In the free zone, there was *Liberté*, founded by Captain Henri Frenay and later called *Combat*; *Libération* created by François de Meutton and *Franc Tireur* set up by Emmanuel d'Astier de la Vigerie. In the occupied zone, the most important group was the civil and military organisation (OCM), followed by *Libération Nord* and the Special Organisation. At the outset, these resistance groups limited themselves to political action, to the setting up of links with England and the relay of information. But the German attack on the USSR gave a boost to this early resistance. The Communist Party entered the fray, bringing with it experience in subversive activities and tough discipline. The communists were the first to take direct action: sabotage and attempts on the lives of German officers.

De Gaulle was quick to realise the advantages of this home resistance. Although he disapproved of the assassination attempts which provoked terrible reprisals, he was determined to organize the movement and to lead it, while at the same time limiting his dealings with the British SOE. In this way it was easier for him to speak in the name of France. At the end of 1940 he instructed Jean Moulin, former Prefect of Eure-et-Loir, who had been brutally treated at the hands of he Germans and dismissed from office by Vichy, to establish a liaison between the resistance movements and the National Committee and to coordinate the activities of the resistance inside France. Hounded by the Germans, Jean Moulin managed to carry out his mission, although not without some difficulty, at the beginning of 1943. He created the MUR (*United Resistance Movement*) which incorporated all the movements including the communists. On 27th May Moulin presided over the first secret meeting of the CNR (*National Resistance Committee*) in Paris, at which all the parties were represented.

The Resistance now began to assume real importance; it claimed the loyalty of tens of thousands of men. The German requisitioning of man power, the STO (Obligatory Labour Service) only helped to swell the numbers. The first *maquis* sprang up and sabotage, especially of railways, became frequent. Apart from the communist dominated groups like the FTP (*Franc-Tireurs Partisans*) there were other groups of a more classical type such as the *Armée Secrète*, formed

99

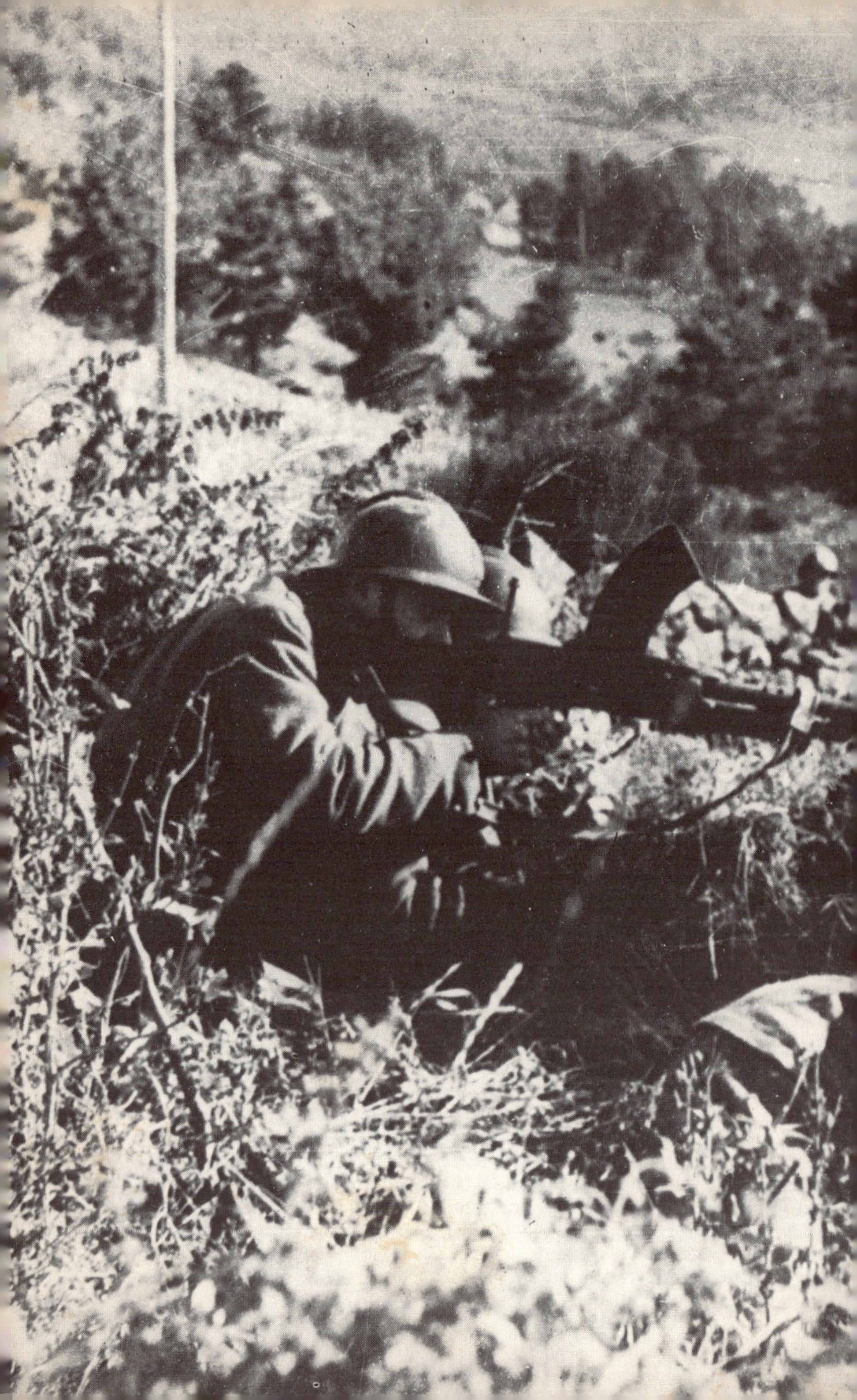

Maquis snipers

Pierre Mendès-France, one of the French politicians who refused to come to terms with the Vichy regime and who eventually rallied to de Gaulle

by ex-officers of the army which had capitulated.

But it was not so much the military aspect of the Resistance which interested de Gaulle at that time. His aim was to make himself the political leader of that section of the population which refused to capitulate and which had taken up the struggle against the enemy. He was leader of those French who were still fighting both inside and outside France. It was a new opportunity for him to embody French legitimacy. At the same time de Gaulle was extending a warm welcome in London to those politicians who had refused to come to terms with the Vichy régime. Among these were André Philip, Félix Gouin, Pierre Brossolette, Max Hymans, and Mendès France. Although some of them were reluctant to do so, he intended to link the parties of the defunct Republic with the Resistance. The CNR included members not only of the resistance movements, but also of the former unions and political organizations.

By incorporating different parties into the Resistance, de Gaulle increased his following but also gave rise to grave misunderstandings in the future. The majority of his parliamentary supporters were men of the Left, fierce opponents of the Vichy régime. They expected the General to re-establish the traditional republican régime. They were more interested in de Gaulle as the opponent of a reputedly totalitarian régime than as a fighter. When André Philip arrived in London he was asked 'what is your opinion of General de Gaulle?' 'I couldn't give a damn about the general,' he replied, 'I have come to join the under-secretary of state for National Defence in the last free, and therefore legitimate, government of the Republic.'

Finally, the socialist deputy declared to de Gaulle: 'General, as soon as the war is won, I shall leave you. You are fighting to restore national greatness, I to build a socialist and democratic Europe...'

With consummate skill, de Gaulle ceased to mention his criticism of the party 'system', which he judged responsible for the defeat of France. Indeed, he began to make overtly 'republican' statements. Léon Blum, former leader of the Popular Front, was so reassured about his sympathies that he sent him a letter from prison in which he wrote: 'I note that you have pledged yourself unreservedly to the principle of democracy and I firmly believe that a democratic state – whatever its constitution and whatever the part played in it by parliament – cannot exist and cannot even be conceived without the existence of political parties.'

But these concessions did not prevent de Gaulle from treating the deputies harshly in private. He said to Bouscat: 'They are ambitious and mediocre. They often get under my feet. But I would hesitate to get rid of them...' He was still convinced that when the time came he would be able to make them obey him: 'A group of resistance movements has been formed in France. This group is led by one of *my* men, a prefect, a member of the National Committee. In this group there are not only resistance movements but also political parties. It has the support of all the leaders: Blum, Herriot, Marin and even the communists. *This group has placed itself under my orders.*'

But there were some who underlined the danger of this alliance of the parties and the Resistance. They felt it might compromise their chances of re-establishing a solid and powerful democratic régime. When he arrived in London, Henri Frenay, the founder of *Combat*, asked the General: 'This organisation the CNR has been formed by political personalities and it will have a political outlook. What will happen if, in a situation other than that in which you find yourself now, its politics are different to yours?'

'I will give an order' de Gaulle replied.

'General', Frenay went on, 'on the military level, we will not question your orders. But it will not be the same in the political domain.'

De Gaulle replied characterstically: 'Well, Frenay, France will have to choose between you and me!'

On this score, the General was still sure of himself. 'France is Gaullist, fiercely Gaullist. She wants de Gaulle', he would frequently say. This was true of many, but was it true of all? While keeping their respect for the Marshal's person, the vast majority of the country followed the General's battle with interest, if only through the intermediary of the radio. De Gaulle was generally considered to be the man placed to represent the country's interests abroad. But once France had been liberated, would he be able to keep the country behind him over the infinitely more delicate problems of domestic politics?

For the time being at least the title of Leader of Fighting France, both at home and abroad – excluding, of course, the struggle being waged in Tunisia by the Army of Africa – gave de Gaulle a privileged position. It was a position that became more comfortable as the unhappy Giraud made ever

Henri Frenay. He founded the resistance group *Verité* which fused with *Combat*

more blunders. Through bad advice he chose to ignore the French Resistance which was, according to him, merely an aggregate of groups with no influence, fighting among themselves, and dominated by the communists. He accepted, at Churchill's request, a modification of the Anfa agreement: from now on, he would no longer hold the 'trusteeship' of French interests except in Africa. He then made the additional mistake of replacing Chatel with Peyrouton as Governor General of Algeria. Whatever the moral integrity of Peyrouton, or his role after the elimination of Laval in December 1941, he had nevertheless been a minister in the Vichy Government, and this was an unforgivable sin in the eyes of orthodox Gaullists. He also accepted the support of André Labarthe and of Admiral Muselier who had broken with the Free French on the morrow of the Saint-Pierre and Miquelon affair and had become a declared enemy of de Gaulle.

In the end, tired of being considered a reactionary and an instrument of Vichy by people in London, Giraud decided to attempt a manoeuvre in the grand manner and outflank de Gaulle's programme. His speech of 14th March, mainly inspired by Jean Monnet, annulled the Vichy legislation, promised a 'democratic' constitution and announced a change of course towards the Left. The result was precisely the opposite of the one he had intended. Although the British press showed satisfaction at this 'conversion', the Army of Africa did not conceal its disappointment at the abandonment of the Marshal's 'National Revolution'. The Moslems were worried about possible concessions to the Jews, who, for their part, were annoyed because the Crémieux decree had not been dropped. Finally, in making the 'first democratic speech' of his life, Giraud gave the impression that he was coming round to de Gaulle's political ideas. It was thus that after 14th March a wave of anxiety overtook Giraud's supporters who now feared a victory for de Gaulle.

In spite of all, Giraud held fast to his political views and in the end it was de Gaulle who agreed to go to Algiers in May, as part of a compromise which seemed to favour his rival. On the basis of a 'diarchy', the two men presided over an Executive Committee, with Giraud still in command of all the armed forces. Why did de Gaulle accept this solution? It seems that he yielded to the pressing invitations of Catroux who persuaded him that time was running out. The victory in Tunisia, in which the Army of Africa play-

Giraud (far right) in Tunis for the victory celebrations, May 1943

ed an important part, had for the time being raised the prestige of his rival. And there were two other successes to his credit: the winning over in quick succession of the French West Indies and Admiral Godfrey's squadron which had been stuck in Alexandria ever since the armistice.

The pressure brought to bear by the Allies also played a part. On 8th May, Roosevelt, still insistent on this 'marriage' between de Gaulle and Giraud, wrote to Churchill: 'The bride's behaviour is more and more intolerable. He is installing his general staff of venomous propagandists in Algiers to sow the seeds of discord ... De Gaulle may be a man of integrity, but he is prey to a messiah complex.' The British Prime Minister, who had arrived in Algiers on 29th May, the day before de Gaulle, said to his friend, General Georges: 'I have given him £25,000,000 and he has said the worst things about England and the United

French troops march past in Tunis

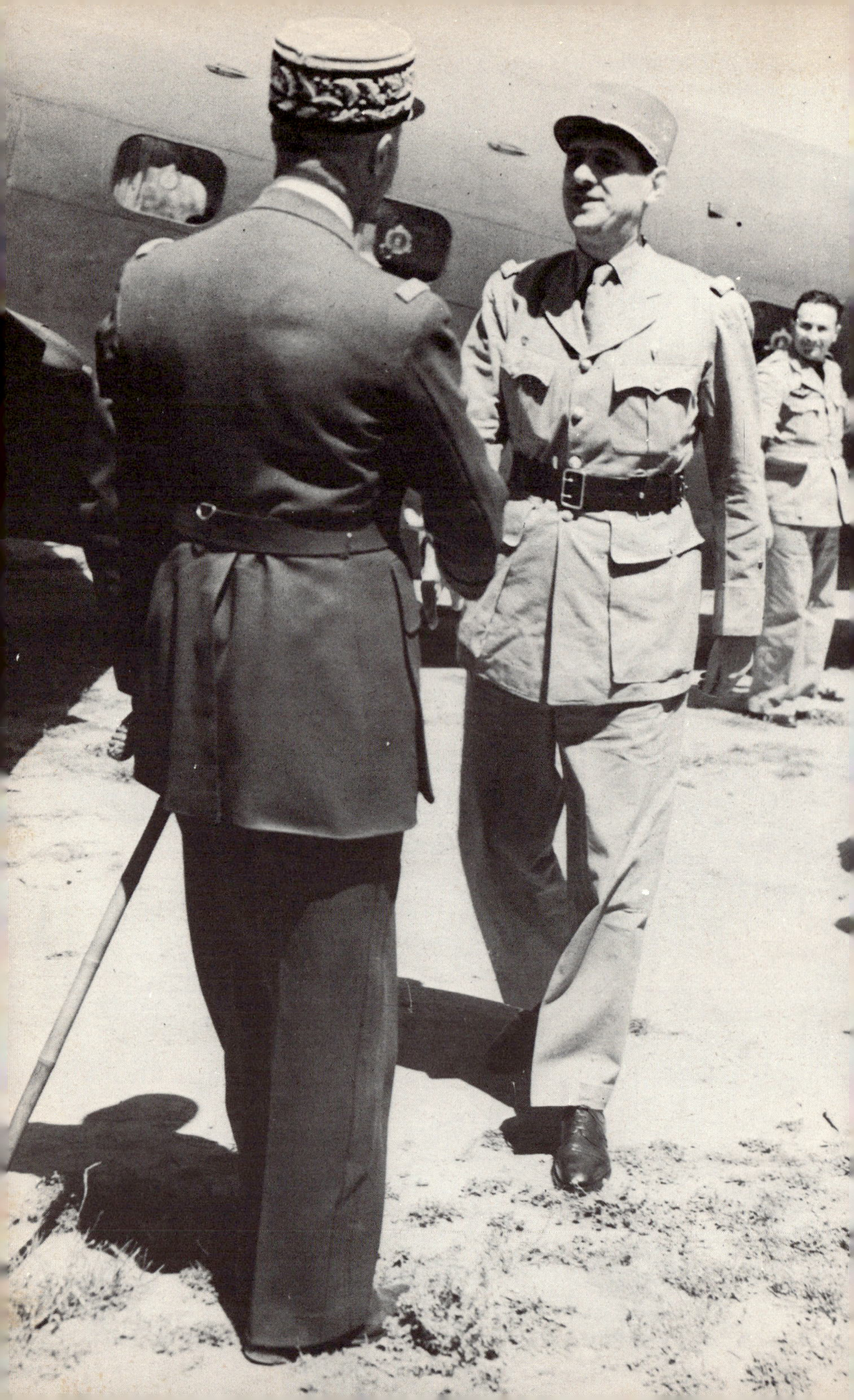

Giraud and de Gaulle meet in Algiers

States. If he returns to London without having come to an agreement with the people here, his position will change.'

The next day de Gaulle arrived in Algiers. Contrary to his expectations, not even the slightest demonstration greeted him. The two men greeted one another drily: 'Bonjour Gaulle.' 'Bonjour Giraud.'

On the 31st the new French Committee for the National Liberation (CFLN) held a meeting. The factions were neatly balanced. Giraud had the support of General Georges and Jean Monnet, de Gaulle of André Philip and the diplomat, René Massigli. General Catroux played the part of arbiter, at least in principle. From then on the two rivals were face to face and, in the course of a tussle that lasted through the next few months, de Gaulle stripped the unfortunate Giraud of all his privileges with astonishing skill. At the very first meeting of the CFLN, de Gaulle demanded the elimination of the 'proconsuls' appointed by Vichy. Giraud refused. The leader of the Free French stormed out, slamming the door behind him. The crisis was on. For a moment Giraud considered deporting his former subordinate to southern Algeria. But he was weary, disillusioned and already under the sway of his adversary's moral ascendancy. He failed to act and the capitulations began.

One after the other, Peyrouton and Boisson, fearing for themselves, handed in their resignations. Noguès was relieved of his duties. A new team in the service of de Gaulle replaced these men. Catroux became the governor general of Algeria, Puaux and Mast were posted to Morocco and Tunisia. At the same time the CFLN was packed with Gaullists who were in the majority from then on. The leader of Fighting France had crossed the first

De Gaulle speaks at Ajaccio after the liberation of Corsica

French mule teams in Italy

hurdle. His rival was isolated, discredited; he had been unable to support the men who had placed their trust in him.

Flushed with this first success, de Gaulle pursued the battle on another field: the incompatibility between the functions of co-president and Commander-in-Chief. Giraud had to make a choice: he dug his heels in. So de Gaulle played a very tricky hand: he resigned. But in spite of Eisenhower's support, Giraud did not dare seize the opportunity. He allowed his adversary to go back on his decision and fell further into the mire of disrepute. He then went to Washington to study the military problems with the Americans. He left the field free for de Gaulle who, on 14th July, Bastille day, made an important speech in which he put himself forward as sole head of government.

As yet nothing was decided, but de Gaulle was biding his time for an opportunity to rid himself of his adversary. It came finally with the liberation of Corsica. At the time of the Italian capitulation on 8th September 1943, the island's position was not clear. An uprising planned by the Corsican National Front (CFLN) broke out, but the attitude of the Italian and German troops was uncertain. With indisputable good judgement, Giraud took advantage of the situation without reference to the CFLN. A landing was made with purely French resources, the island was reoccupied, the Italians disarmed, and the Germans obliged to beat a hasty retreat.

But de Gaulle would not stand for the way the affair was carried out. 'I am hurt and annoyed,' he told Giraud, 'at the way you have behaved towards me and the government in concealing your action . . . ' On 1st October he wrote to the CFLN: 'The conditions under which all the operations surrounding the liberation of Corsica were prepared and executed, almost entirely without reference to the National Liberation Committee, show yet again that the Committee, as it has been constituted and as it actually functions, is not capable of playing the role of an organ of government.'

De Gaulle then set a trap into which his adversary was to fall headlong. He proposed a ruling that the Committee would henceforward have only one president who would be elected for one year and be eligible for re-election. Giraud was confused. On 9th November, de Gaulle, by virtue of a decision taken by the Committee three days earlier, asked all the members of the CFLN to resign so that a new team might be set up. Unaware of the trap that was being set, Giraud accepted . . . But on the new list, neither his name nor those of General Georges or Doctor Abadie appeared. Giraud then declared that he was the victim of an unfair trick and Georges snapped 'Shut up! You are making a fool of yourself!'

Now the former governor of Metz had no title other than Commander-in-Chief of the military forces. But de Gaulle could not resist taking from him even this last function. On 4th April 1944, he had himself made 'leader of the Armies' by the CFLN and on the 8th he abolished the functions of Commander-in-Chief by a simple decree. As compensation, he offered Giraud the title of Inspector General of the Armies, but it was a title devoid of any substance and purely honorary.

A letter, not lacking in flavour, accompanied this offer: 'General, in the situation in which our poor country finds itself you cannot, for purely personal reasons, take a negative attitude towards those who have taken on the terrible task of government in the face of the enemy and in the midst of foreigners. One must, when one is General Giraud, set an example of abnegation and, I must add, discipline (in the loftiest sense of the word).'

Giraud was filled with bitterness but he refused with dignity the offer of a first class burial and retired to his villa, to disappear completely from the political scene, the victim of his truly disarming naiveté and lack of political sense. With a touching frankness he later admitted his failings in his memoirs with their revealing title: 'One aim, victory'. Nevertheless, thanks to him a revived French army fought courageously in Italy. General Juin's expeditionary force landed in the autumn of 1943 and fought fiercely in the Appenines and at Belvedere, to the north of Cassino. In the spring of 1944, it played a decisive role in the breaking of the Gothic line and the march on Rome. On 5th June 1944, General Juin entered the Eternal City alongside General Clark. But the cruel ways of politics denied General Giraud the one joy he felt to be his due: 'to return to France at the head of the soldiers who had just liberated France.'

General Juin after the fall of Rome

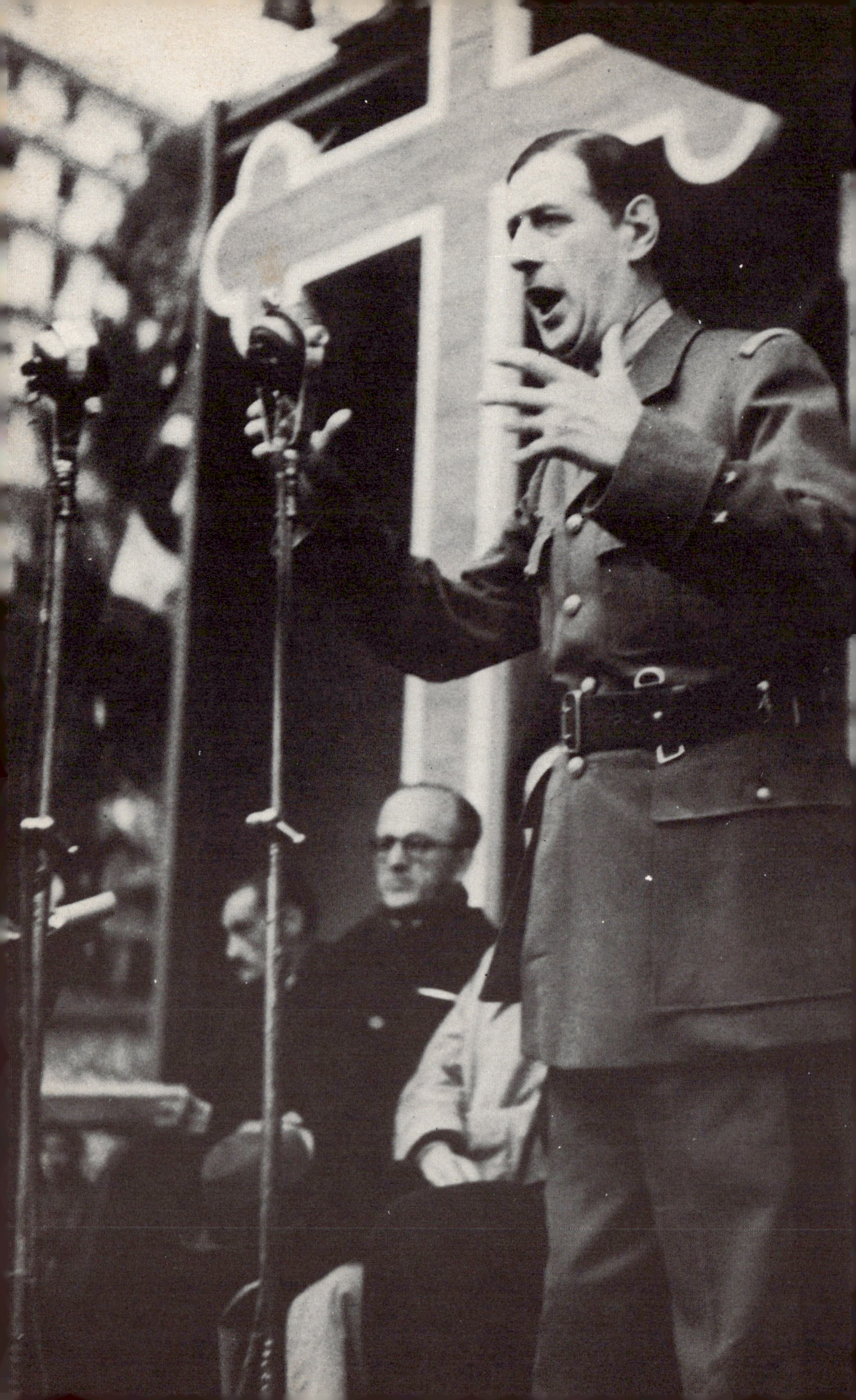

The future in the balance

By November 1943, almost a year to the day after Operation Torch, de Gaulle was sole master in Algiers. From that time on, without altering his cold and lofty bearing, he ceased to behave like a partisan and became more and more the true statesman.

He faced a double problem in the liberation of France, an event which showed every likelihood of taking place in the course of 1944. First of all he had to swell the Committee, making it as representative as possible so that it could become the future Provisional Government of France. He then had to plan the liberation not only from the military but also from the political and diplomatic points of view.

After the elimination of Giraud as co-president, the National Liberation Committee was enlarged and strengthened. Apart from faithful followers of de Gaulle like Catroux, Tixier, Pleven, d'Astier de la Vigerie, Capitant, Diethelm, and Frenay, it included deputies who had refused positions offered by Pétain in 1940: Henri Quenille, Pierre Mendès France, André Le Troquer, Louis Jacquinot, and technocrats like Jean Monnet and René Mayer. This council, which met twice a week in the Summer Palace, did not follow parliamentary rules. It was still the General who made the decisions.

But the appearance of a Consultative Assembly confirmed a democratic and, on the whole, a republican leaning. In principle, this assembly of eighty-four members was meant to represent those sections of opinion which had refused to accept defeat: forty representatives of the home resistance and twelve representatives of the resistance abroad, all nominated by the CNR; and twelve general counsellors from the Algerian departments. In fact the problems of the moment permitted only forty-seven to take part in the debates.

But for all that, the Assembly confirmed the 'legitimacy' of the General. Even though his role remained purely 'consultative', it 'marked the beginning of the resurrection of the French representative organisation.'

It was a decisive turning point. These organisations in Algiers marked the return to 'republican legality' and in his speech of 14th July 1943, the General uttered the word 'Republic' for the first time since 1940. A year later, on 25th July 1944, while the Battle of Normandy was raging, he was more explicit: 'As for the political order, *we have chosen*. We have chosen

De Gaulle speaks in Algiers, 1943

Above: Francois Billoux and *Below:* Fernand Grenier, two communists appointed by de Gaulle to the Liberation Committee

democracy and the Republic.'

It would be natural to question this idea of 'choice', in contradiction to the silence, the reserve, or even the declarations of the previous years. In 1940, the General had still betrayed that he had monarchist leanings while at the same time that he fell under the strong influence of Christian Democracy. In the first few months of his stay in London, his hostility had been directed equally against Vichy and the Third Republic. The sterile party game and the lack of real power was the root of the defeat. He said to one of his closest colleagues: 'There are two words which I will never say: Republic and Democracy.'

'What will you say to Churchill and Roosevelt?' he was aked.

'I will say liberty', he replied.

Certain aspects of the 'National Revolution' did not displease him. He frequently said, 'There is good in Vichy, without the Germans.' In his memoirs he added: 'In the realms of finance and economics, the technocrats of the Vichy régime behaved, in spite of set-backs, with undeniable skill; and the social doctrines of the 'National Revolution' – corporate organisation, work charter, family privileges – had some ideas which were not without attraction.'

He was not the only one at this time to feel attracted towards a strong, essentially monarchist régime, one which attempted to resolve on a nationwide scale the traditional conflict between capital and labour. On the BBC certain well-known Free French personalities, while condemning the armistice, nevertheless paid homage to certain actions of the Vichy régime. General Leclerc, when invited to put forward suggestions for the future government of France, recommended: 'Suppress all the political parties. Promise to retain some of Marshal Pétain's measures, in particular those which reinforce central authority and benefit the family.'

The de Gaulle of 1940-41 was not

averse to a Salazar-type formula. In his ideas on the future constitution of France, the Russian Ambassador, Maisky, detected an 'odour of fascism'. De Gaulle, he said, would develop the theme of a corporative Chamber with agricultural, industrial and commercial representatives. A strong executive power would be reserved for military and diplomatic questions. It was 'neo-bonapartism'.

There was certainly nothing democratic about the way the Empire Defence Council or the CFLN were run. On his arrival in London, the deputy, Félix Gouin, discovered a 'sort of copy, in miniature, of the Pétain government.' The slogan 'Liberty, Equality, Fraternity' did not appear on any official document. Later, the General looked back on this period with nostalgia: 'That sort of monarchy which I once espoused . . .'

The democratic trend which began in 1943 can be explained in several ways. The General realised that it would be impossible to resume the Vichy experiment, with its overtones of defeat. The war was developing in a way which made sacred the victory of the democracies and he was well aware that this meant that an authoritarian régime was out of the question for the time being. Furthermore, the Vichy experiment was still condemned by the zealous support of the army old guard, while resistance to the occupation had been a phenomenon of the Left. The participation of the USSR in the war further modified the balance of forces and did much to rehabilitate the communist party whose members now embraced an iron patriotism. In order to associate the party with the war effort, de Gaulle decided in March 1944 to appoint two communists to the Liberation Committee: Francois Billoux as Commissaire d'Etat and Fernand Grenier as Air Commissaire. Finally, the reasons for de Gaulle's drift to democracy were purely tactical. To isolate Giraud, de Gaulle was forced to appoint veteran deputies to the Committee or to the Consultative Assembly. These survivors of the Third Republic were only a tiny minority among the new men, but their experience and the prestige attached to the vote of 10th July 1940 gave them considerable influence and helped to create a state of mind which recalled the days of the Republic.

For the time being, the Consultative Assembly bowed to de Gaulle on questions of general order, but there was one point on which it would not give way: the punishment of the Vichy leaders. On 3rd September 1943, the Liberation Committee decided 'to assume responsibility, as soon as circumstances permit, for bringing to justice Marshal Pétain and all those who took part in the pseudo-governments formed by him, who capitulated, made an attempt on the Constitution, collaborated with the enemy, delivered French workers into the hands of the Germans and used French forces to fight against the Allies and the French who continued the struggle.'

A threat now hung over the heads of thousands of Frenchmen who, through the course of troubled times, found themselves accused of treason and collaboration. On 20th October, an Order decreed that justice would be meted out by a special military tribunal with 'far-reaching powers'. In spite of protests from Roosevelt and Churchill, the arrests began. The victims were governors of the colonies, like Peyrouton and Boisson, or senior officers like General Bergeret, Darlan's former Chief-of-Staff, and Admiral Derrien, commander of the base at Bizerta who was condemned to death and executed. In all, these measures affected nearly 300 civil servants, magistrates, and teachers in North Africa. The Army of Africa was judged 'infected' and was not spared. Almost all the generals were eliminated in one way or another. General Juin only narrowly escaped disgrace. Nor did the purge spare those of more modest rank: one officer in the Italian Expeditionary Force received

Pucheu, one of the men who suffered the inevitable purge of Vichy ministers. He was tried and shot on 22nd March 1944

an order to appear in Algiers on the very day he fell at the head of his men.

By far the most important case – indeed it became a test case – was the trial of Monsieur Pucheu. Pucheu, Minister of Industrial Production, then Minister of the Interior at Vichy, had decided at the end of 1942 to break with the Marshal's régime. He had crossed to North Africa with the authorization of Giraud who thought it wiser to put him under house arrest in southern Morocco. On 10th August 1943, the National Committee decided to arrest him. His trial before the military tribunal began in March 1944. Several charges were levelled against him: instigating enlistment for a foreign power at war with France, producing texts with 'bloody repercussions', placing the French police at the service of the occupation authorities. The gravest charge was that he collaborated with the Germans in the drawing up of a list of hostages at Nantes and Chateaubriand.

Pucheu was found guilty and condemned to death on 16th March. De Gaulle refused a pardon although he admitted that his trial had been a political one. 'We are living through a nightmare,' said the General, 'which owes its origin to the fact that certain people saw fit to lay down their arms before they had run out of resources; this led to the dreadful policy of collaboration and all its consequences. I do not doubt that certain people acted in good faith and I am sure that Pucheu was one of them. I am even sure that he was one of those who did their utmost to oppose the Germans and to safeguard France's interests as much as possible. We are not judging his intentions. The facts lie before us and the tribunal has passed judgement on the political realities. No one forced Pucheu to enter the government, no one forced him to stay there.'

Pucheu was shot on 22nd March. De Gaulle gave the order to the firing squad himself. This affair helped to weaken the position of Giraud who, in the words of Pucheu himself, was 'discredited as a soldier and as a man'. Above all, it generated a first wave of uneasiness among the public and revealed how 'Reasons of State' could operate.

The passions unleashed by the first purges and the trends which emerged in the Consultative Assembly ultimately gave de Gaulle cause for anxiety. He feared that the Resistance fighters might take the Liberation as an excuse for a reckoning between the traditional Right and the Left, a pretext for the destruction of institutions that were the backbone of the state. In his Memoires he noted the Resistance fighters' mistrust and even hatred for everything administrative, regular, official . . . '

Several months before Operation Overlord, he stepped up his warnings. If the Vichy régime was really and truly considered null and void, and if the decision to re-establish the 'authority of the Republic' constituted an 'obligation', there was nevertheless an important nuance. It was not merely a matter of restoring the institutions of the 'Third', even if the Republic had never officially been abolished, but of setting up the 'Fourth'. On 3rd November 1943 de Gaulle declared in Algiers: 'France has suffered too many trials and has learned too many lessons, her own and others, not to want profound change. She must act in such a way that, tomorrow, national sovereignty can assert itself completely, unmarred by intrigue and the corrupting influence of any coalition of private interests. She wants the men to whom she gives the responsibility of governing her to have sufficient means to accomplish their duty. They must have the force and the continuity necessary to impose the supreme power of the state on all within the nation's boundaries, to pursue ends worthy of her name outside.'

Finally, on 25th July 1944, he stated: 'It must be said that if the government intends to carry out, in metropolitan France, the necessary eliminations . . . it has no intention whatsoever of wiping out the great majority of servants of the State, most of whom, during the terrible years of the occupation and the false régime, sought above all to serve the public interest in the best way possible. The running down of certain French institutions and of certain of their members is easily done, but it is too often unjust or exaggerated. Besides, the public powers have the servants they deserve and it is by setting an example of competence, impartiality, and responsibility that they stand the most chance of being served as they wish.'

If circumstances were ever to prevent the General from establishing the strong and stable régime that he envisaged, he would always have one recourse: appeal to the people.

It was thus that, on the eve of D-Day, the main problem obsessing the General was the re-establishment of the State. A new administration would have to be established in advance so that, when the time came, it could take the baton from Vichy.

A whole series of orders governed the exercise of authority during the Liberation. Seventeen 'commissaires of the Republic' took over regional administration. Prefects and sub-prefects were secretly appointed to replace those of Vichy. Finally, as a concession to the Resistance, a 'Liberation Committee', set up in each department, would assist the prefect.

The purge was not forgotten. The most 'notorious' defendants would be judged by a High Court in Paris. But in each court of appeal there would be 'courts of justice' set up to judge the crimes and offences of collaborators. Finally, there would be a complete reorganisation of the press. Any paper which had continued to appear more than a fortnight after 11th November 1942 in the southern zone would be abolished.

All these measures were intended to provide continuity and impress the Allies. In this way, 'among the French people, before the Allies, and in the midst of the defeated enemy, the

The *Maquis des chasseurs Alpins* who opposed not only the Germans but also the collaborators

authority of the State would appear, complete, responsible and independent.' In the same spirit, the order of 3rd June 1944 declared that the National Committee would be called the 'Provisional Government of the French Republic'.

At the same time, de Gaulle attempted to reinforce his control over the Resistance and to make it the instrument of his policies. The disappearance of Jean Moulin, arrested and tortured to death by the Germans in May 1943, caused some wavering. In the end, it was Georges Bidault, a Christian Democrat, who became president of the CNR in which the communists held three seats out of six. In the Military Action Committee, the COMAC, they had a majority proof of a growing independence. In order to keep in touch de Gaulle appointed Alexandre Parodi delegate general in Metropolitan France. The Algiers Committee appointed 'regional delegates' subordinate to three 'national military delegates' of whom the most important was twenty-nine-year old brigadier-general, Jacques

Chaban Delmas. This hierarchy was intended to strengthen Gaullist influence and to counteract that of the communists. At the same time, de Gaulle appointed General Koenig, the 'hero of Bir Hakeim', as head of all the military formations of the Resistance which took the name of French Forces of the Interior (FFI). The Francs Tireurs and the Communist Partisans retained a considerable degree of independence.

A few months before the D-Day landings, the Resistance doubled its activity. *Maquis* sprung up in the mountain regions: the Massif Central (Mont Mouchet) and the Alps (Vercors). Sabotage and assassination attempts multiplied. The Germans replied brutally with punitive expeditions and summary executions. But the resistance was not limited to the struggle against the occupation: it was aimed particularly at collaborators, especially after Darnat's Militia joined the Germans in suppressing resistance uprisings. The communists did not hide their intention of promoting social unrest. In certain regions, like the south-west, the uneasy beginnings of a real civil war began to appear.

Despite the provision of arms, munitions, and radio stations, the purely military action of the Resistance was still of little interest to General de Gaulle. After the landing,

Rifles are distributed to the Fighting French from salvaged equipment

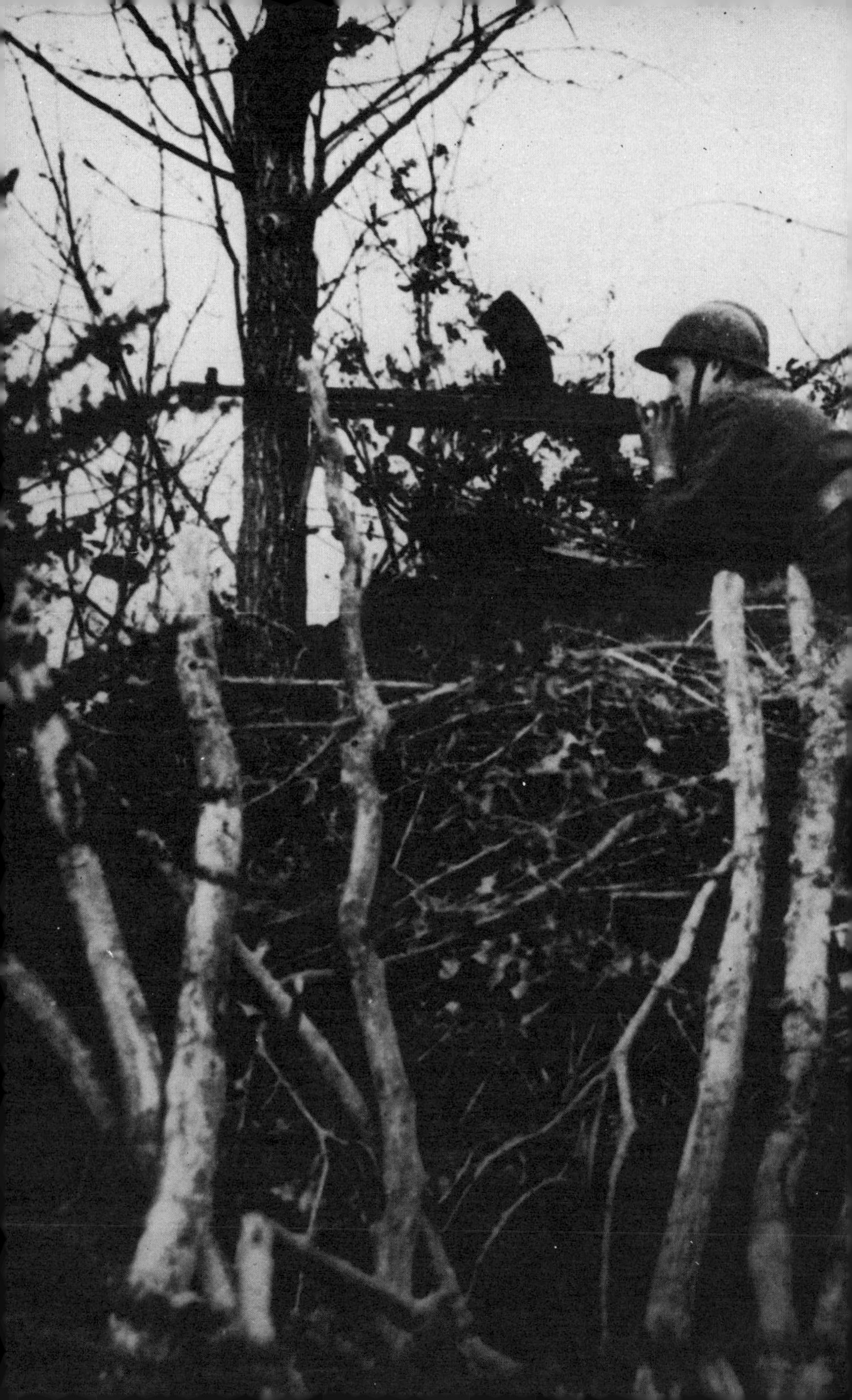

A maquis outpost at St Nazaire

the FFI were warned to proceed carefully. The Vercors *maquis* even experienced the horror of abandonment. For the General, the Resistance was a force to keep in reserve until the time came to launch the attack. Since 1942 he had been developing the idea of the 'insurrection'. 'The national liberation cannot be divorced form insurrection,' he declared. 'But this general uprising should not be premature. It will come when the German front is broken, after a fairly long period of stabilization. Then the insurrection will take on the appearance of an immense tidal wave sweeping the enemy troops into retreat and heralding the advance of the Allied forces. France must liberate *herself*.'

On this point, de Gaulle was hoping that French troops would be in the vanguard of the Allied armies, or at least at the focal points. It was for this reason that he was totally opposed to General Juin's idea of following up the Italian offensive in the direction of Brenner and the Llubljana pass. In so far as his forces were concerned, he took the American point of view and favoured a landing in the south of France. After 15th August he insisted to de Lattre de Tassigny that the First French Army should lead the operations up the Rhone Valley.

Although de Gaulle was still unaware of the general outline and the date of Overlord, he nevertheless insisted that the 2nd Armoured Division, his favourite unit, should be involved in the decisive operation and that the privilege of 'liberating' Paris should be reserved for him. All these measures had only one aim: to impress the 'foreigners' and to force the Allies to recognize the authority of the Algiers Committee, now the Provisional Government.

But on the eve of the most vital operation of the war, de Gaulle's relations with the Allies were at their worst. His bitterness was ill-concealed; he could not forget what had been said to his representative in Washington, by the diplomat, Dunn: 'Why can't General de Gaulle get it into his head that all that remains for him is to take command of a tank division?' The Algiers Committee had not been associated with the Italian capitulation. Above all, the General could not stomach the Allied – and particularly the American – intentions with respect to the regions of liberated France. The shadow of Amgot (the Allied administration in Italy) hung over France. De Gaulle constantly brooded over the suggestion made by Roosevelt to André Philip in November 1942: 'as far as I am concerned, France does not exist politically speaking, until the moment when elections provide her with representatives . . . We are training a group of politico-military specialists who will ensure the administration of France until democracy has been re-established . . .'

De Gaulle's mood was getting blacker each day. The smallest incident took on dramatic proportions. It was thus that, on the eve of the landing, when the British banned all coded dispatches between London and Algiers for reasons of security, the General's anger led him to order his representatives in London to cease all contact with the British authorities.

A new storm was now about to break. On 4th June, the General arrived in England at the invitation of Churchill. That afternoon, de Gaulle accompanied by Koenig, Béthouard and Vienet met the British Prime Minister on his train near Portsmouth. Bevin, Eden and Marshal Smuts were present at the meeting and Churchill announced that the D-day landings would take place that night. De Gaulle stood stock still and his brow darkened. He had been told only at the eleventh hour. The conversation turned to the administration of the liberated territories and

De Lattre de Tassigny, whom de Gaulle insisted must lead operations in the Rhône valley

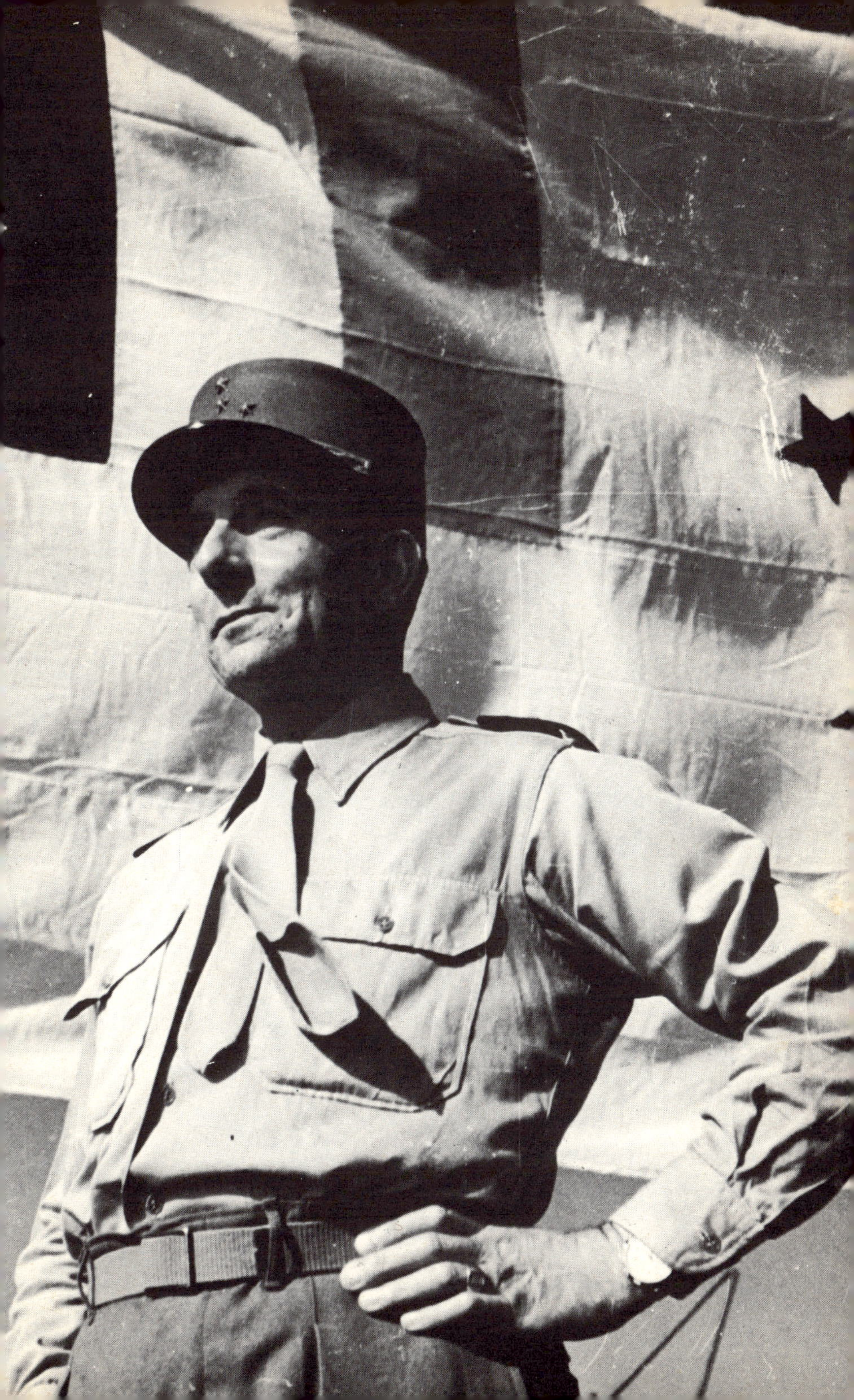

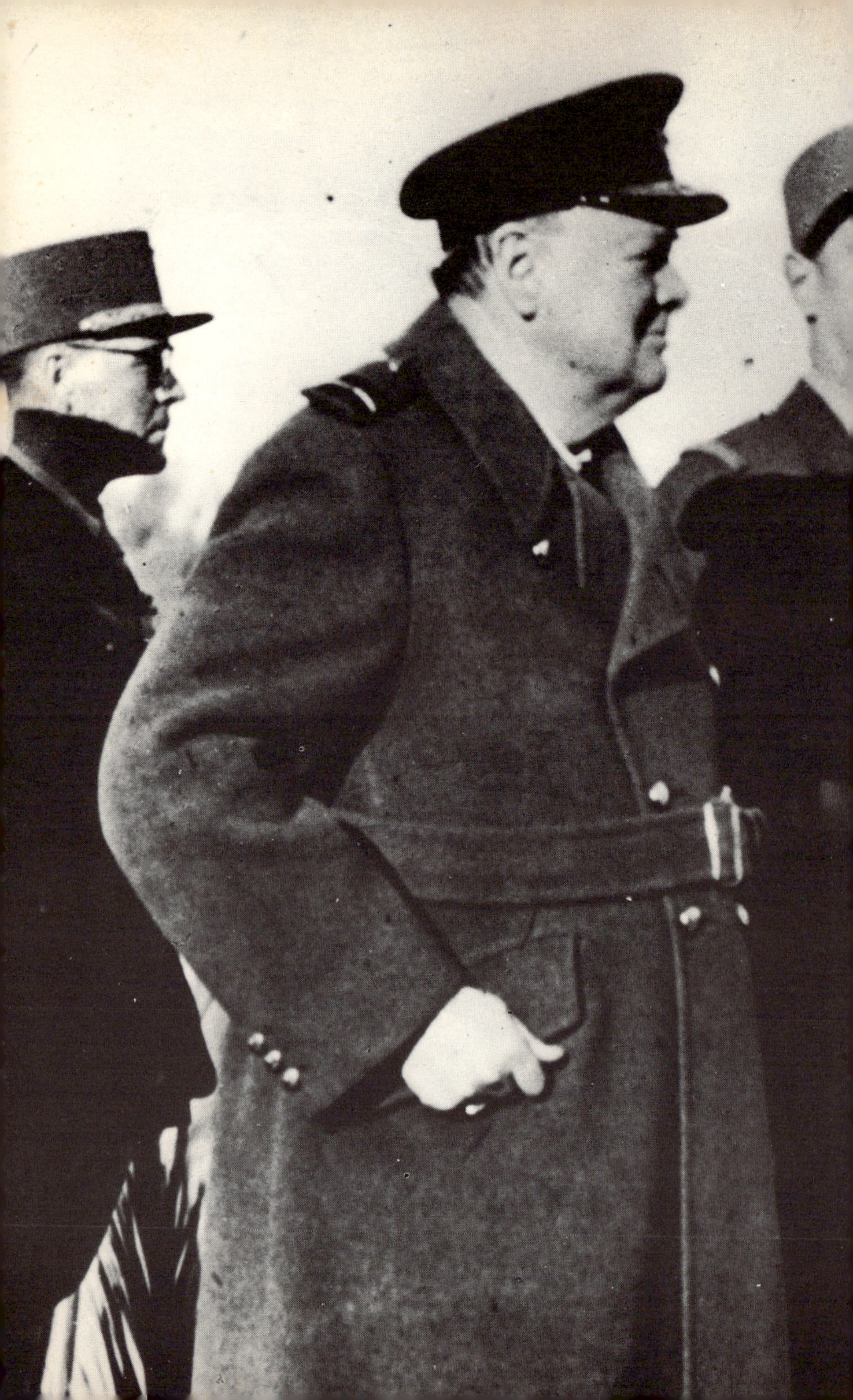

it was then that the explosion occurred. 'Do you imagine that I have to place my candidature for power in France before Roosevelt or before you? The French government exists! I have just heard that the troops who are about to land are carrying so-called French money, printed abroad, that the government of the Republic absolutely does not recognize . . . I expect that, tomorrow, General Eisenhower will proclaim that he is taking France under his authority. In these conditions, how do you expect us to deal with you?'

Furious at this outburst, Churchill let fly a famous tirade: 'Know this, General de Gaulle, each time that we have to choose between Europe and the open sea, I will always be for the open sea. Each time that I have to choose between you and Roosevelt, I will always choose Roosevelt.' Bevin then tried to ease the atmosphere, but de Gaulle, beside himself with rage, carried on: 'We are here only to discuss military affairs: politics and the administration are our own affair . . . And don't talk to me about your counterfeit money.'

That same evening, in an angry mood, Churchill drafted a letter to de Gaulle ordering him to leave British territory. Eden toned down the message. But before the day was over there was a new affront and another outburst from the General. Eisenhower showed him the main outlines of Operation Overlord and handed him the text of the proclamation he intended to make to the French people. It was a precise reflection of Roosevelt's own ideas. There was no mention of the 'Provisional Government of the Republic', and the Commander-in-Chief of the Allied Forces invited the French to 'carry out his orders'. Furious, de Gaulle refused an invitation to dinner and forbade the departure of his liaison officers.

Churchill and de Gaulle meet at Marrakesh

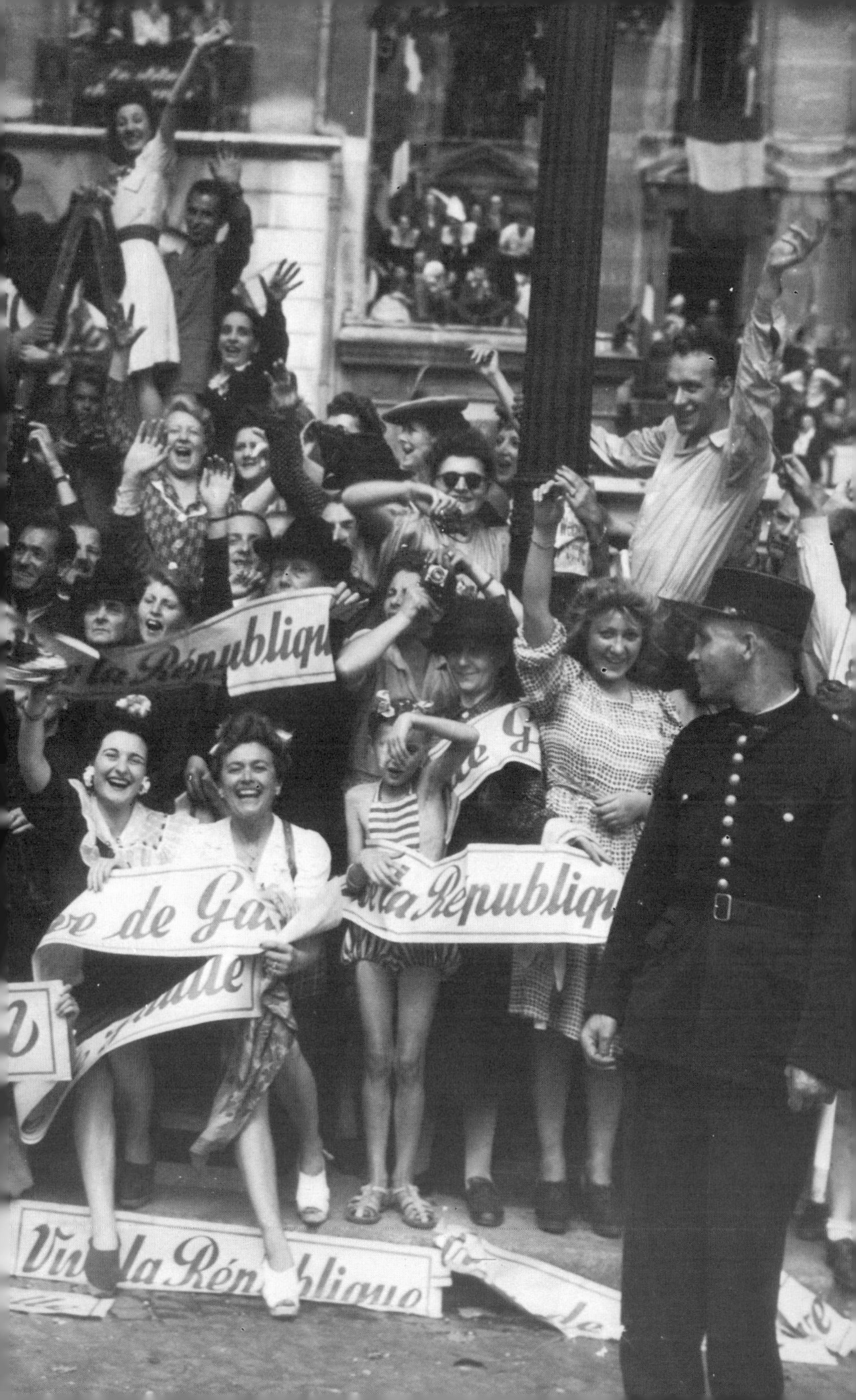
la Républiqu
re de Ga
la Republiqu

Victory

At dawn on 6th June the operation which was to decide the outcome of the war began. If it failed, Overlord could not be repeated in less than a year and the Germans would have then plenty of time to concentrate the bulk of their forces in the East and perhaps to reach a separate peace with Russia. Nevertheless, de Gaulle agreed to broadcast a message that evening: 'The decisive battle has begun ... Needless to say, it is the Battle of France and it is France's battle ...' There was one particularly significant sentence: 'The orders given by the French government and by the French leaders that it has appointed, must be followed exactly ...'

14th June was the decisive day. De Gaulle boarded the torpedo boat *La Combattante* at Plymouth and landed near Courselles. He soon arrived at Bayeux. The little town had been spared by the fighting and had had little to complain of from the occupation. The Vichy sub-prefect was still in office and the Marshal's portrait still occupied a place of honour, a week after the Liberation. At first, people showed surprise: the General's size, his gestures, and his expression were disconcerting. But Maurice Schumann took it upon himself to create a welcome for the General. De Gaulle had his first immersion in the crowd, shook hands, nearly 3,000 hands it is said, mounted a platform, congratulated the inhabitants on their attitude during the occupation – there were not even 100 members of the resistance in the region – and struck up the Marseillaise.

That evening the General re-embarked, satisfied with his day. Popular acclaim was as good as a plebiscite. 'The proof has been given.' The Vichyite sub-prefect hastily disappeared. He was replaced by a local resistance fighter bestowed with the titles of Commissaire of the Republic and military commander. The Allies were presented with a *fait accompli*. In the days which followed, de Gaulle inspected French troops in Italy, had an audience with Pope Pius XII, returned to Algiers and on 6th July, arrived in Washington. Hiding his true feelings, Roosevelt received him amicably but he angered the general by sketching out a map of the world as it would be after the war – dominated by a big four from which France would be excluded. After the meeting, the President remarked that 'as far as

Paris celebrates its liberation

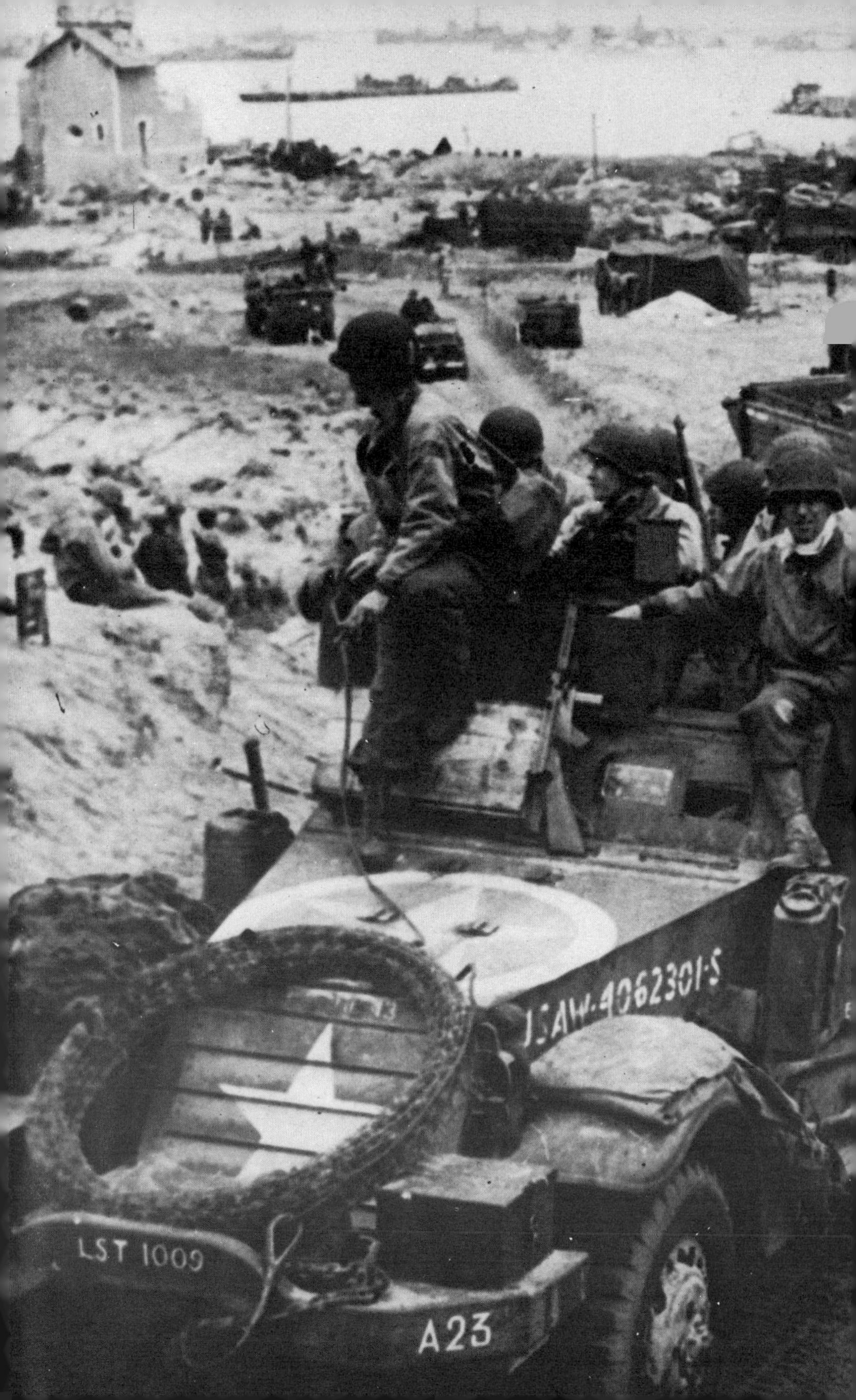
LST 1009
A23
4062301-S

D-Day landings. Supplies move inland from the beaches

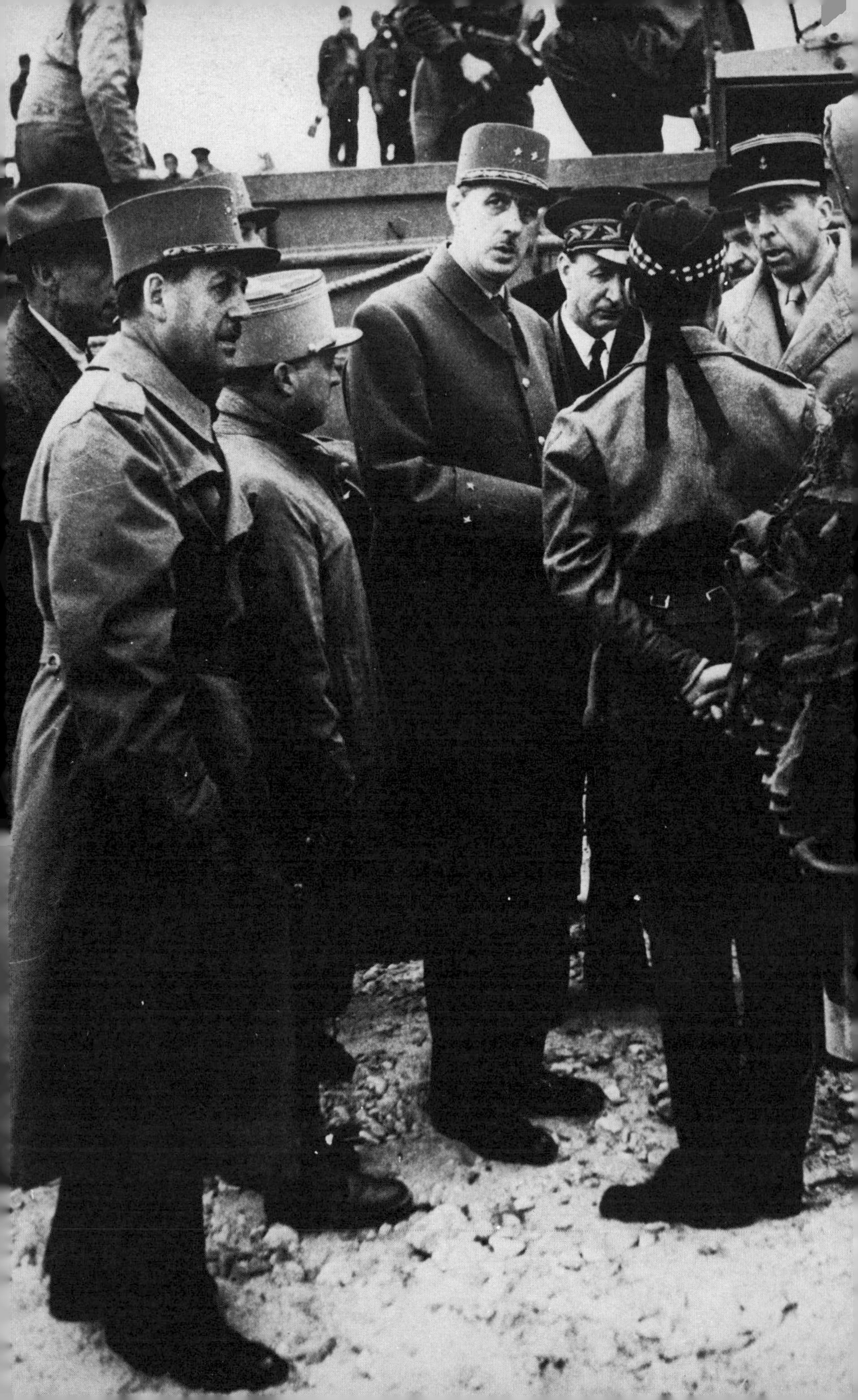

De Gaulle addresses the people of Bayeux

future problems are concerned, they seem quite manageable so long as France is treated on a world level. He is very touchy when it comes to France's honour. But I think that he is essentially an egoist.' De Gaulle ended his visit with trips to New York and Canada. Everywhere he went he received a very warm welcome. The Epilogue came on 12th July: that day the American government recognized that 'the French Committee of National Liberation is qualified to exercise the administration of France'. It was still not 'recognition' of the Provisional Government; that did not come until October. But it was nevertheless a great victory.

There was still one battle to be fought: to win the recognition of the French people and to mount the 'liberation of Paris'. Until August, de Gaulle showed interest in only one thing: the fierce fighting at the bridgeheads. But after the breakthrough at Avranches and the threat of encirclement posed to the German armies, he realized that the decisive hour, so eagerly awaited since 18th

14th June 1944. De Gaulle lands on French soil

June, was drawing near. The time had come to liberate Paris, to conquer the heart of France.

On 20th August de Gaulle landed at Cherbourg and went immediately to Eisenhower. Paris had risen against the occupying forces the day before, on the initiative of 'Colonel' Rol, leader of the FFI and a communist. He had taken this action despite the warnings of Parodi and Chaban-Delmas who believed that his actions were precipitate. Sporadic fighting broke out between the Germans and the Resistance. Next day, through the offices of Mr Nordling, the Swedish consul, General von Choltitz agreed to a truce lasting not more than twenty-four hours. On the 22nd the fighting began again. Once more it was the communists who were behind it, for they hoped to manoeuvre themselves into a commanding position while they could. Barricades sprang up all over the city.

At that time, a rapid occupation of Paris was not part of General Eisenhower's plans. He intended to outflank the capital from the south and the north. De Gaulle feared that the uprising would be crushed or that the communists might win. He did not hide his discontent and threatened to take back the Leclerc division and put it into action alone. When Eisenhower was told what was happening on the 22nd, he decided to step in and send General Gerov's corps to the help of the capital, along with Leclerc's 2nd Armoured Division and the 4th American Infantry Division.

On the evening of the 24th, these forces arrived in the southern suburbs of Paris where they gave violent battle and suffered heavy losses. That night a detachment of the 2nd Armoured Division, led by Captain Dronne, managed to sneak into the heart of the capital and reached Notre Dame and the Hôtel de Ville. The news spread like lightning. All the bells began to peal. At the Hotel Maurice the officers of the German general staff wondered what was going on. General von Choltitz told them: 'It is the liberation of Paris.'

The next day, 25th August, the Americans in the eastern quarters and the French in the western quarters reduced the German strongholds. By the evening the German commander of the occupying forces agreed to sign a cease-fire in the presence of Leclerc and 'Colonel' Rol.

It was at that moment, at about 4.30 in the afternoon, that de Gaulle made his entry into the capital, wearing the impassive mask of the statesman. He reproached Leclerc for having accepted Rol's signature on the act of surrender, an action which he said showed 'unacceptable tendencies'. His first act was to pay a symbolic visit to the Ministry of War where nothing had changed since 10th June 1940. 'Nothing is missing, except the State.' Next, he reviewed the police at the Prefecture and only then did he decide to go to the Hôtel de Ville where the members of the CNR had been waiting for him for two hours. He made a short speech about the restoration of the State. The General refused to let the members of the Council be presented to him. He also refused somewhat drily to comply with Bidault's request that he should appear on the balcony of the Hôtel de Ville and proclaim the Republic. He did not bother to explain that this would be tantamount to recognizing the existence of Vichy. He contented himself with saying 'The Republic has never ceased to exist . . . I myself am president of the government of the

6th July. De Gaulle arrives in Washington to see Roosevelt.

Eisenhower and de Gaulle meet in Normandy

Republic. Why should I go and proclaim it?'

Nevertheless he appeared to the assembled crowd outside the window and was greeted with wild enthusiasm. But the grand finale would not take place until the next day. In the early afternoon, the General arrived at the Arc de Triomphe. He refused a military parade. Preceded by four tanks and an usher, followed at a respectful distance by the members of the CNR, Generals Juin, Leclerc and Valin, de Gaulle decided to walk down the Champs-Eylsées, in order to give a 'friendly' and 'fraternal' impression. One has only to see the films of the time to understand that for the General this was the most unforgettable hour of his life. Wildly acclaimed by the vast crowd that lined the Champs-Elysées, it was there that he tasted the revenge for four years struggle, insult, and doubt.

This demonstration of national unity was momentarily marred by an untimely burst of gunfire, which broke out first in the Place de la Concorde and then on the parvis of Notre-Dame giving rise to dreadful panic among the onlookers. What really happened has never been discovered. It might have been the desperate action of isolated militiamen or Germans, the famous 'roof snipers', lack of discipline among certain members of the FFI whose rifles had gone off accidentally, or provocation on the part of communists who had decided to maintain a subversive climate. This last is the General's view, as expressed in the *Mémoires*. No one knows the truth.

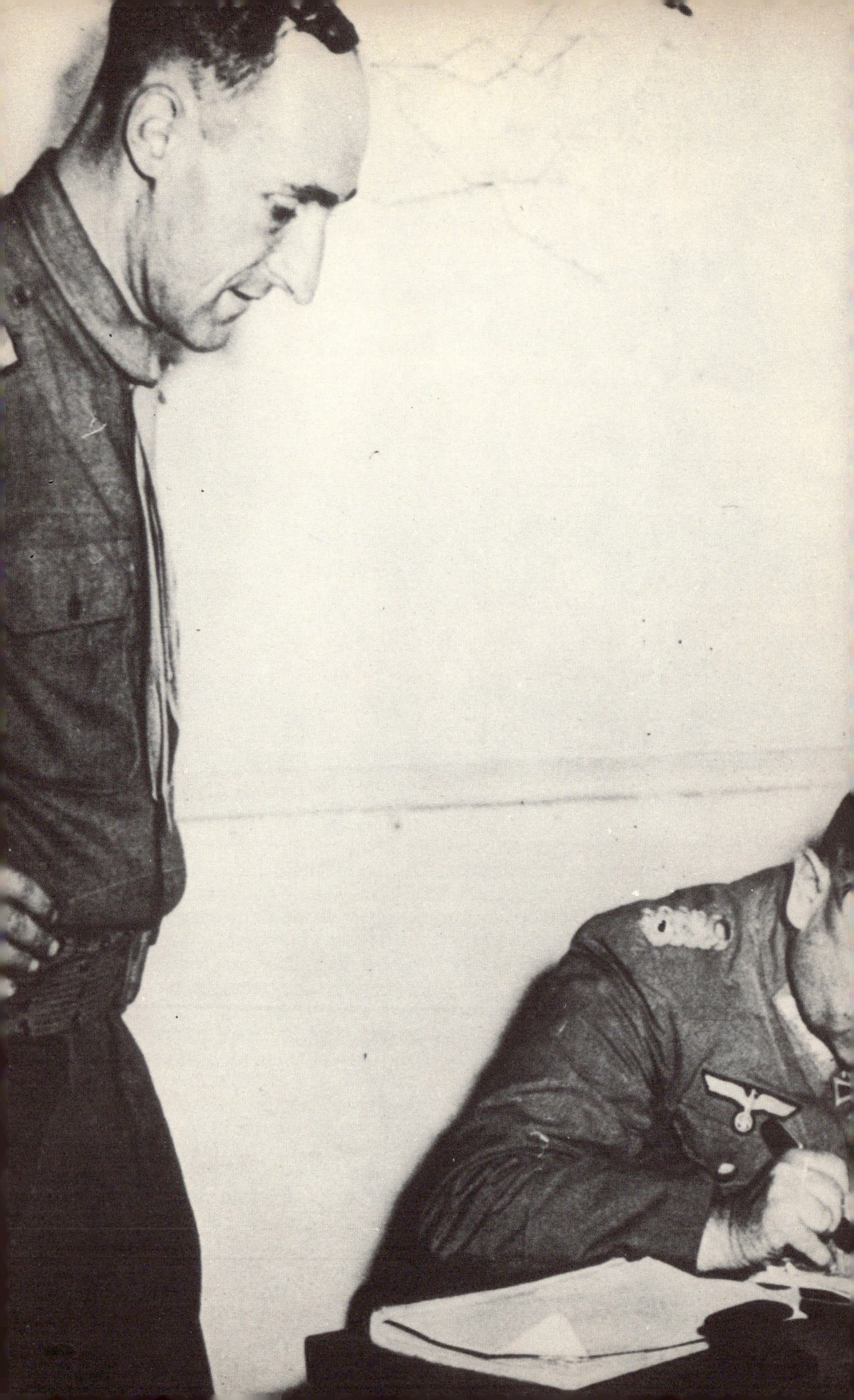

General Dietrich von Choltitz, Commandant of Fortress Paris, signs the surrender to the Allies

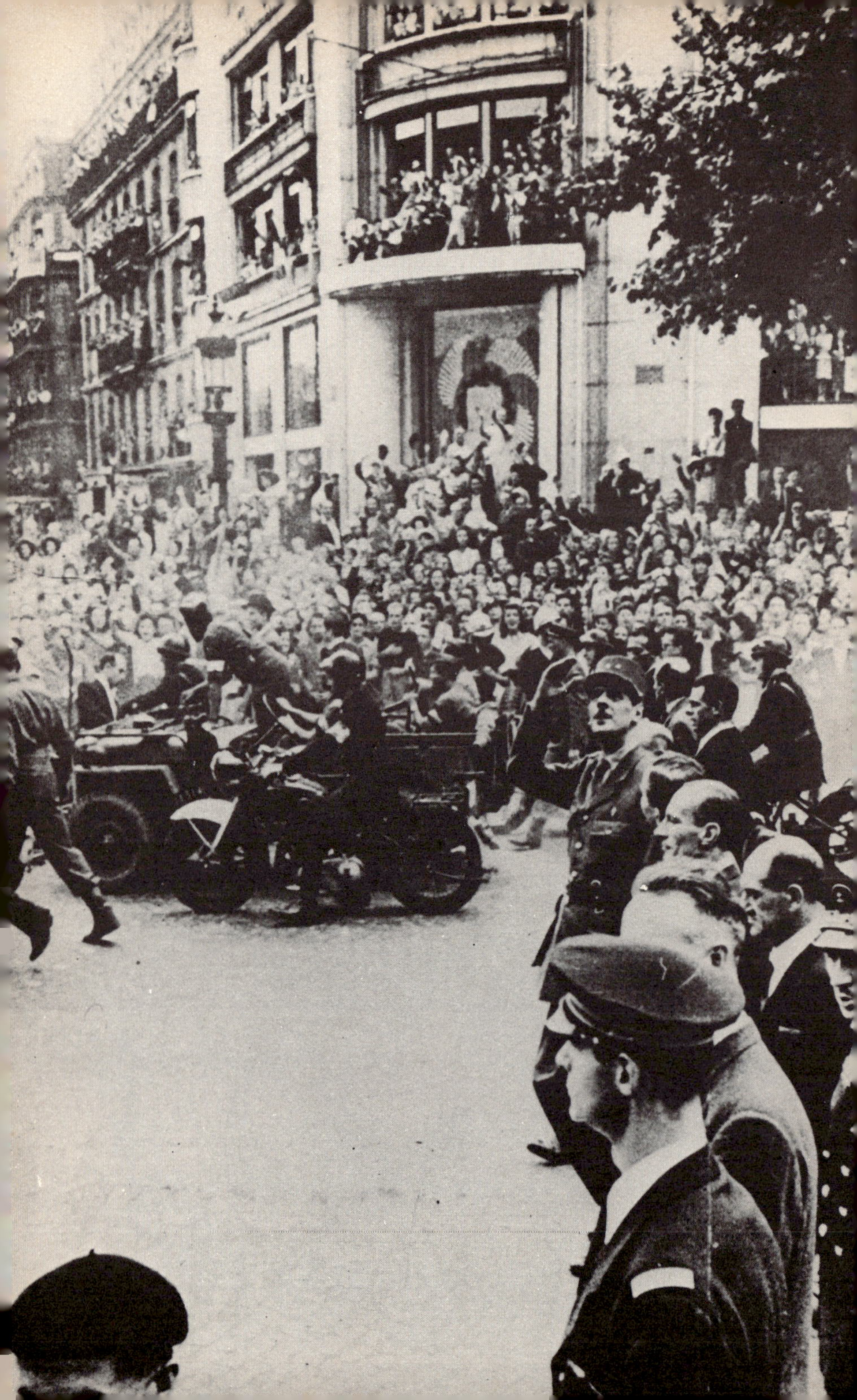

People cower as snipers open fire when de Gaulle arrives at Notre Dame

The incident did not stop him from going into Notre-Dame where, in the midst of the tumult – shots were being fired in the cathedral – de Gaulle struck up the *Magnificat*.

The day was a success. De Gaulle had received the blessing of the people of Paris and had been assured of the support of the whole country. He had achieved his long-cherished aim: he was the incarnation of French legitimacy. The last obstacles had been crushed. On 12th August, in a laughable attempt, Laval, the political old-stager, freed Herriot from German imprisonment and unsuccessfully attempted to persuade him, as President of the Chamber, to take on the leadership of a transitional government. As for the old Marshal, before being arrested by the Germans and sent to Belfort and then to Sigmaringen, he sent the following message to Admiral Auphan,

De Gaulle walks down the Champs Elysées from the Arc de Triomphe

former Secretary of State for the Navy: 'I empower Admiral Auphan to be my representative to the Anglo-Saxon high command and eventually to make contact on my behalf with General de Gaulle or his qualified representatives, in order to find for the French political problem at the time of the liberation of the territory, a solution which will prevent civil war and reconcile Frenchmen of good faith...'

De Gaulle did not hear of the Marshal's last message until the evening of the 25th August. He read it slowly, 'filled with unspeakable sadness'. But, 'in the circumstances,' he later recalled 'this emotion could not rank with reasons of State. 'It is I who represent legitimacy' he said,' 'Because, at the end, it was to de Gaulle that Pétain turned, I can reply only with my silence.'

135

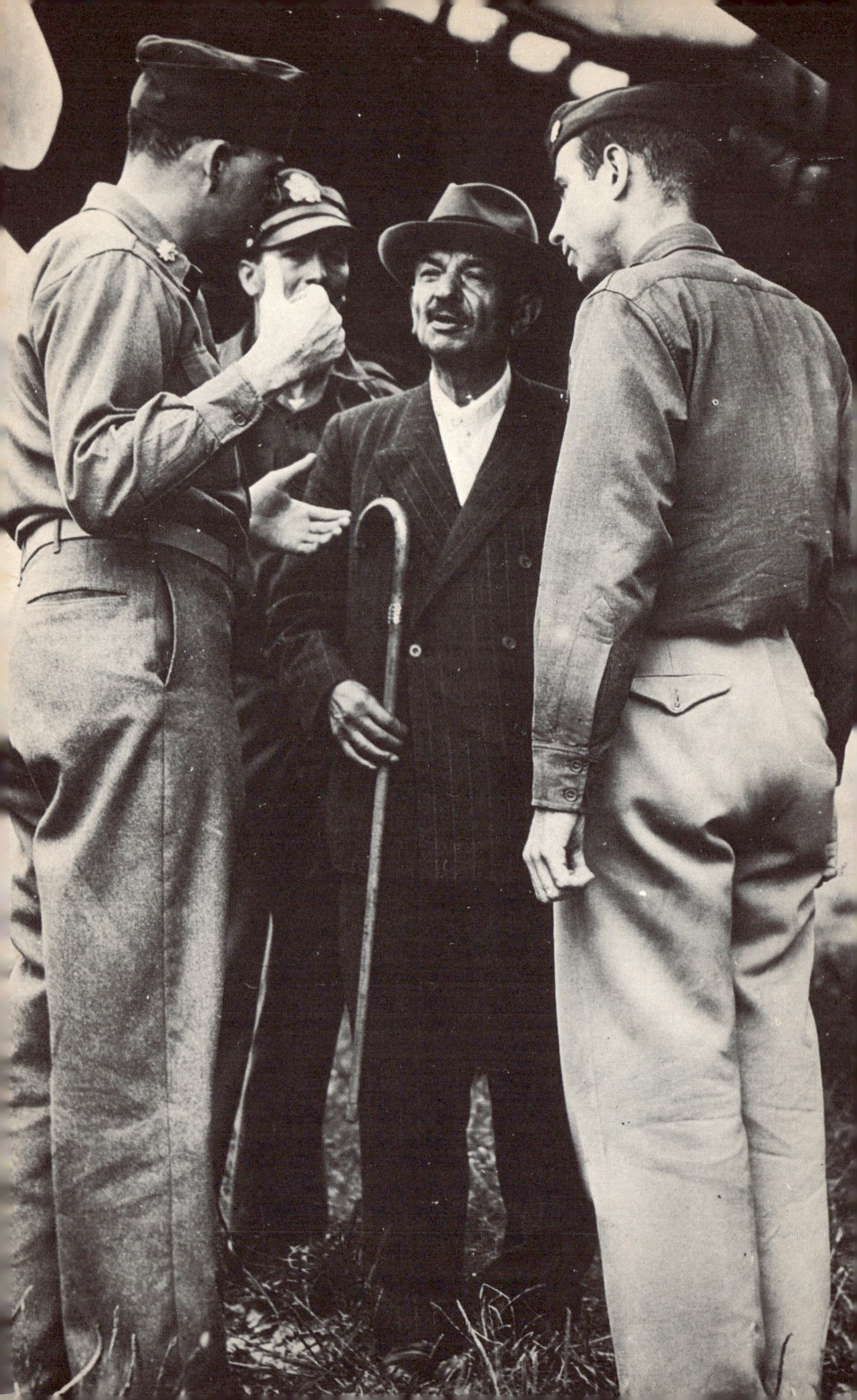

The tedious peace

After his moment of glory a triple task awaited de Gaulle: to re-establish order, to continue the war and to secure his political future.

The re-establishment of republican legality was now a matter of pressing urgency. Already on 26th August, the General was struck by the subversive atmosphere which prevailed in the capital. For this reason he decided to keep the 2nd Armoured Division within easy reach of Paris for a few days. He also asked Eisenhower to lend him two American divisions on a temporary basis, to make 'a show of force'. The Allied Commander-in-Chief acceded to his request and sent two of his biggest units to Paris. 'This parade, coinciding with the plan of operations in that sector was perhaps the first example in history of troops organizing a parade in the capital of a great country and taking part in a pitched battle the same day.' Then de Gaulle had thousands of uniforms distributed to the FFI in the Paris region. They now constituted the 10th Division and were immediately sent to the eastern regions in step with the Allied advance. The objective was to give a 'regular' appearance to the army of the interior. As communications were re-established between the departments and the capital, de Gaulle watched over the reinstatement of a legal administration. Despite the coolness the élites had shown towards him, on 12th September he organised a meeting at the Palais de Chaillot of more than 4,000 representatives of the great State bodies and employers' organizations. At the same time as warning them of the far-reaching reforms that would be necessary, he spoke reassuringly about 'freedom of speech' and 'freedom of enterprise' and he urged his audience 'to strive for greatness'.

De Gaulle intended to quash any attempt at subversion on the part of the communists and to carry out the necessary social and economic reforms while keeping the structure of the nation intact. But in fact, the state of the nation varied considerably from one region to another. France was divided into two distinct parts. First there was the France which had been crossed by the victorious Allied armies, marked out roughly by two great lines from Normandy and Provence which met on the northern and eastern frontiers. In these departments, despite the in-

Laval is captured in Austria. He was tried and executed for treason

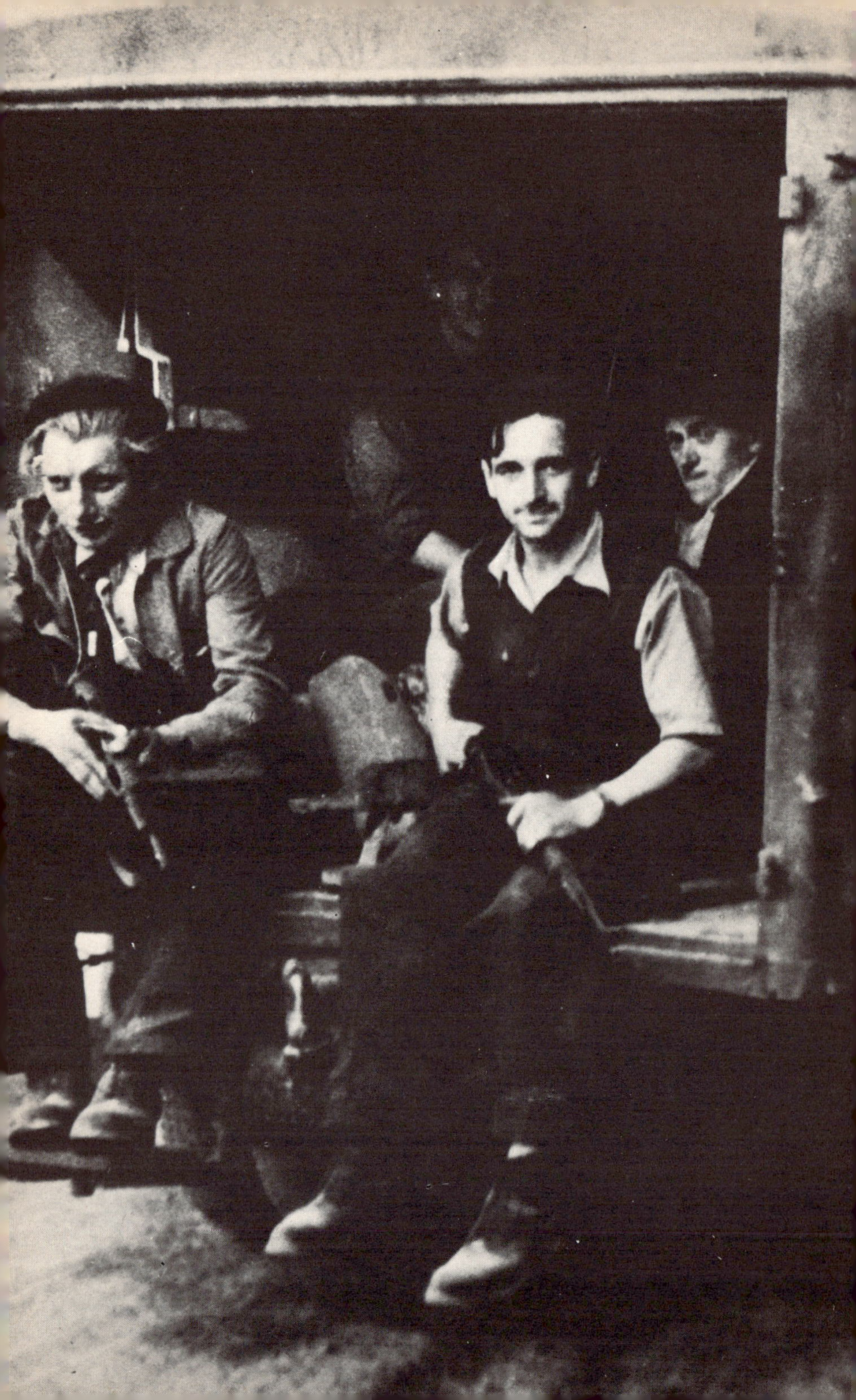

Maquis and Free French out on patrol in Normandy

Maurice Thorez, Secretary-General to the French Communist Party. Condemned to death in 1939, he returned to France from Moscow in 1945 under an amnesty

evitable excesses, order reigned and the new administration could be sure of taking over from Vichy without much difficulty. But elsewhere, in the Massif Central, the South West, in the departments untouched by the Allied troops, the situation was revolutionary and in places there was a real 'red terror'. For the most part, the 'Liberation Committees' were dominated by the communists who were raising 'patriotic militia'. These regions were the scene of numerous summary executions of known collaborators, but also of 'notable' landlords, businessmen, and members of the professions. It seemed that in a third of France, the communist party, rehabilitated by the resistance and under the camouflage of fierce patriotism, were seeking to re-establish the 'dictatorship of the proletariat'.

In the autumn de Gaulle undertook a tour of the great towns in the south and south-east, hoping that his prestige and popularity alone would re-establish law and order. He was enthusiastically received everywhere but he also found great anxiety among the élites and the administrations. On the whole this tour had beneficial effects. Besides, although the General refused to send French troops to the south-west, he took advantage of German elements in the 'Atlantic pockets' to send a great many irregular formations with communist leanings.

In fact, real peace did not come until the beginning of 1945 with the dissolution of the famous 'patriotic militia'. The price paid might seem high. The secretary general of the Communist Party, Maurice Thorez, who had been condemned to death for 'desertion in the face of the enemy' in 1939 and had fled to Moscow, was allowed to return to France on 27th November 1945, under an amnesty. On 21st January 1945, before the central party committee at Ivry, Thorez, to everyone's surprise, condemned the maintenance of the militia: 'these armed groups had their *raison d'être* before and during the occupation against the Nazis and their Vichy accomplices. But the situation has now changed. Public security must be ensured by the regular forces and the police, constituted for this reason. The civil guards and generally speaking, *all* the irregular armed groups must be disbanded now.'

Thorez now set himself up as a valuable auxiliary of the State. His watchwords were totally unambiguous: 'make war', 'set up a strong French army', 'reconstruct industry rapidly', 'unite'. It is difficult to place an interpretation on what amounted to a *volte face*. One must consider General de Gaulle's personal actions, and one must also take into account the presence of American troops, who would certainly not have tolerated subversive activity behind their backs. But above all, one must consider the 'directives' sent from Moscow. For the time being, Stalin wanted to encourage anything which would accelerate the defeat of Germany. It is also

The debris of the German retreat

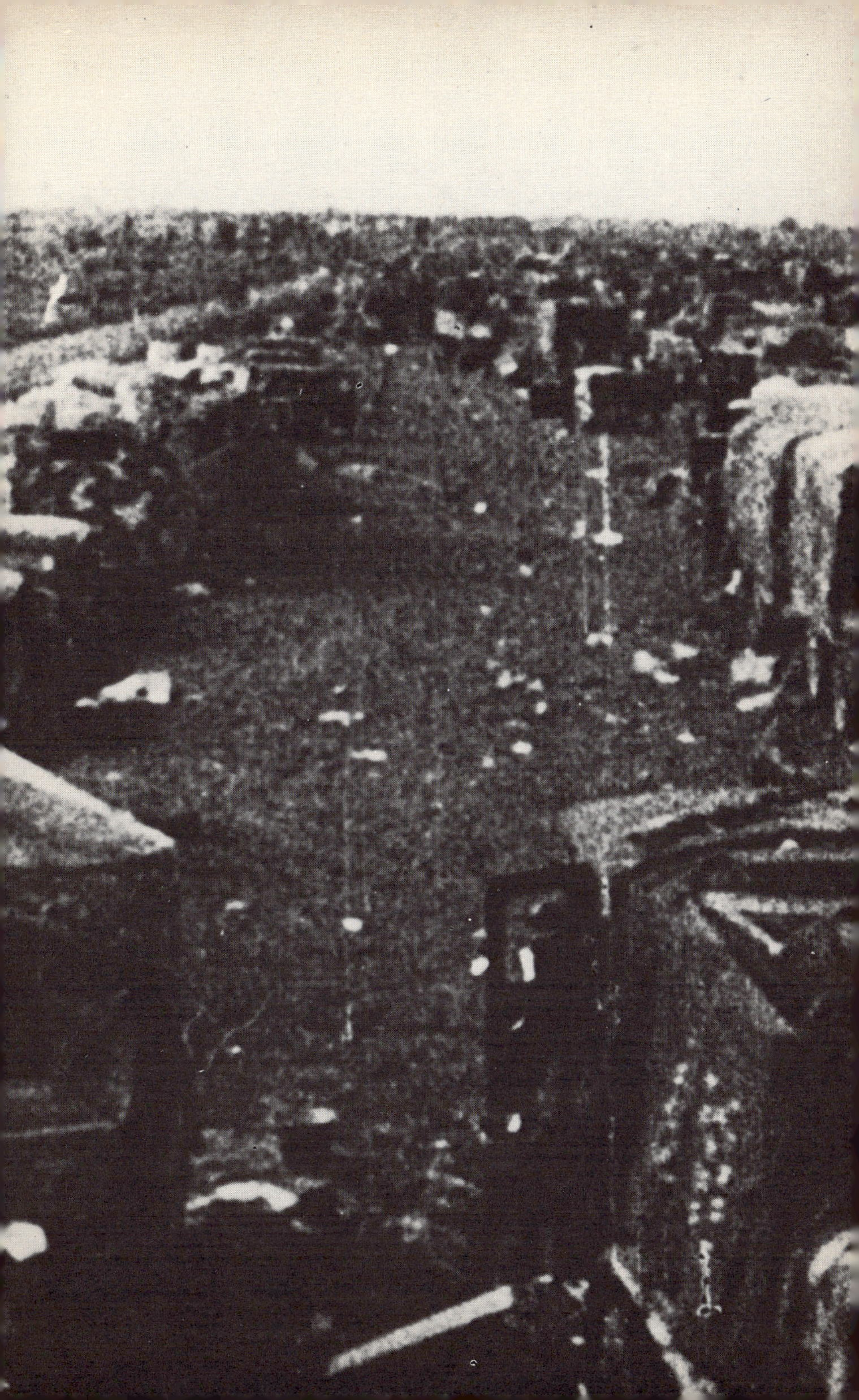

likely that with his customary circumspection, he did not want to risk the danger of a revolution in Western Europe the day after the Yalta agreement. Eastern Europe alone was a rich enough prize to digest. Whatever the reason, the militia agreed to disperse, not altogether happily. For the time being, the communist party was content not to 'scare anyone off', and to profit from the prestige won by the USSR to attract the maximum number of 'sympathizers'. The communists intended to take an option on the future.

So, by the beginning of 1945, the problem of order seemed to have been solved. The General had unquestionably played a central part in the return to legality. But for the moment de Gaulle's attention was concentrated on the conduct of the war and problems abroad. He naturally intended France to regain her position as a great world power. This aim could only be achieved if the country had a powerful army of about fifty divisions. At that time, General de Lattre de Tassigny's First Army was fighting courageously with Patch's group of armies in the southernmost Allied front, facing the Vosges, and Alsace. During an extremely harsh winter and facing an equally tough adversary, these troops managed to liberate Mulhouse, took part in the recapture of Strasbourg and finally, at the beginning of 1945, completely wiped out the 'Colmar pocket'.

On the whole the amalgamation of the Free Forces, the 2nd Armoured Division, the 1st Free French Division and troops originally from the Army of Africa, was effective despite certain residual frictions. At the same time an 'amalgam' was made of more than 50,000 FFI, not without some trouble. But attempts to build up a number of large French units met with Allied resistance. The Allies believed that this would run counter to their hopes for a rapid end to the war, then, during the autumn, serious logistical difficulties gave rise to political misgivings as well. Roosevelt wondered whether de Gaulle might not intend to re-establish the French presence in the Far East as soon as the war was over. In the end, the dream of a powerful French army did not come to fruition.

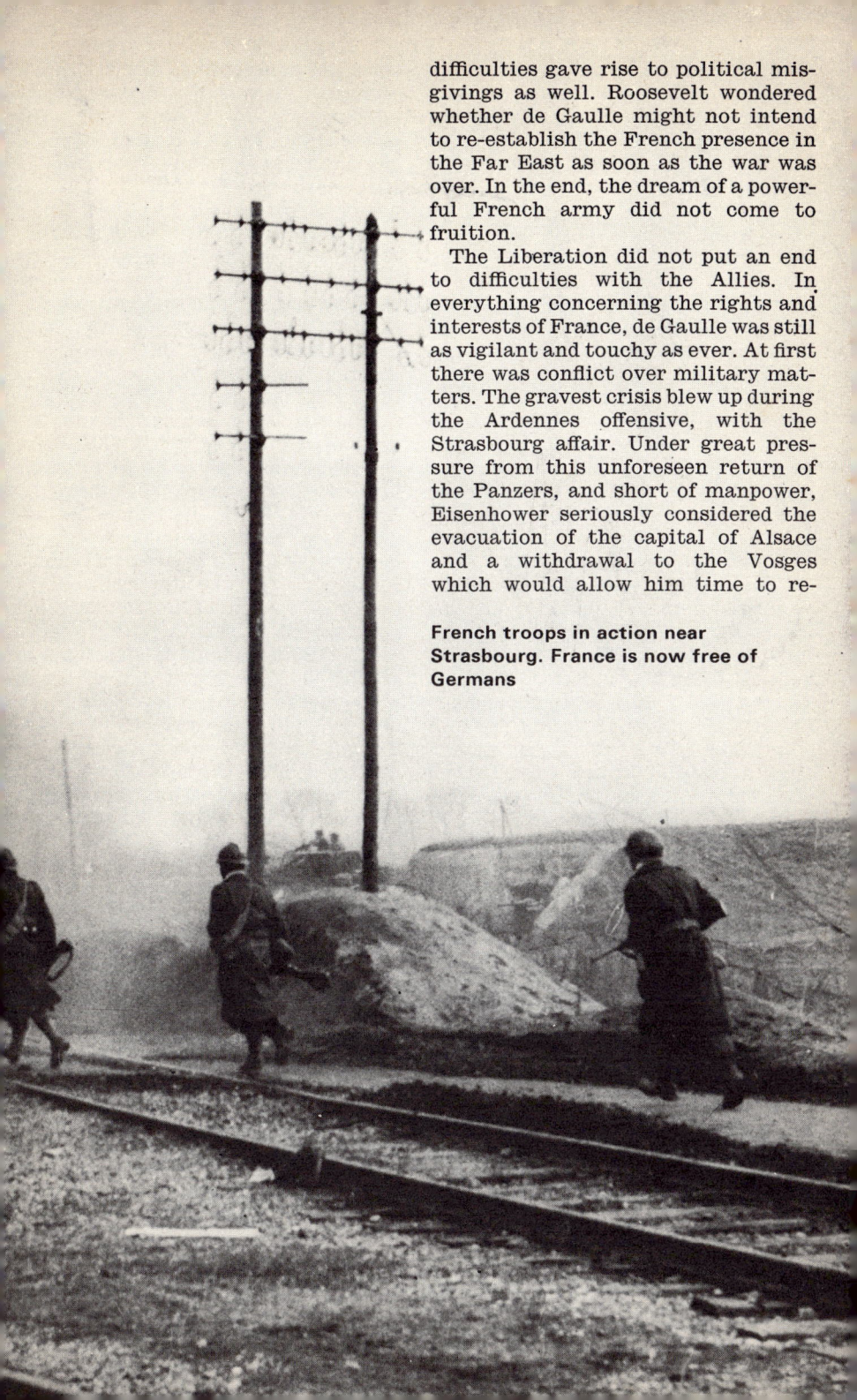

The Liberation did not put an end to difficulties with the Allies. In everything concerning the rights and interests of France, de Gaulle was still as vigilant and touchy as ever. At first there was conflict over military matters. The gravest crisis blew up during the Ardennes offensive, with the Strasbourg affair. Under great pressure from this unforeseen return of the Panzers, and short of manpower, Eisenhower seriously considered the evacuation of the capital of Alsace and a withdrawal to the Vosges which would allow him time to re-

French troops in action near Strasbourg. France is now free of Germans

cover two divisions for the Battle of Bastogne. The consequences of such an event would obviously be grave for the population of Strasbourg. Informed of the situation, de Gaulle, in keeping with his character, immediately brandished his sword. He threatened to withdraw from the Allied command the use of the French ports and railways. The crisis was serious enough for Churchill to come to the continent. Finally, Eisenhower realised the seriousness of the repercussions in France and even in Germany if he abandoned Strasbourg. He agreed, with good grace, to go back on his decision. Two further incidents, although less far-reaching, occurred in the spring of 1945, over the occupation of Stuttgart by French troops, and their refusal to evacuate the high valleys of the Italian Alps.

To a great extent, these military conflicts were feed-back from the disappointments in diplomacy suffered by de Gaulle. The General suffered from the ostracism of which France was a victim. He condemned the idea of a post-war world ruled by a 'Big Three'. This took no account of the interests of France even though she represented, if one includes her Empire, a total of a hundred million people. Besides this, the Allies refused to listen to his views on the eventual dismemberment of Germany and a separate status for the right bank of the Rhine. Finally, de Gaulle considered the absence of France at the Yalta and then at the Potsdam conferences an insult. He denounced the conferences as 'secret and tortuous palaver'. This was the origin of his snub to Roosevelt in refusing to reply to an invitation to Algiers from the president, because it was 'in sovereign French territory'. De Gaulle would not accept France's absence from decisions concerning the future of the world.

The Allies' behaviour caused him to attempt a rapprochement in the east with the Soviet Union. It was also part of his deliberate plan not to give complete adherence to any system of alliances. It was the origin of the famous trip to Moscow where he arrived on 2nd December 1944, a complete stranger to the Russians. His meeting with Stalin bequeathed posterity with one of the finest pages of the *Mémoires*. The General confessed that he had been seduced by 'this great Tsar . . . with his mysterious charm' and he left an unforgettable description of the banquet at the Kremlin. The Moscow discussions resulted in a treaty valid until 1964, but its results were paltry.

De Gaulle did not find Stalin the counterweight he expected. The Soviet colossus refused point blank to adopt his views concerning Germany. At Yalta, Stalin did not hide his indifference to France, possessor of hardly more than a dozen divisions. In return de Gaulle refused to recognize the Lublin Committee, and only agreed to send a liaison officer to the Polish communists. He was sailing close to the wind; a break with Moscow was just around the corner. But this strategy worked. Perhaps the most tangible result was the order Moscow sent to the French Communist Party after Thorez's return.

In spite of everything, France undoubtedly received compensations: the possibility of temporarily exploiting the Saar mines and an occupation zone in Germany and in Austria. These concessions were made at Churchill's prompting since he was worried about a political vacuum in Europe. Besides this, de Lattre de Tassigny just managed to get France in on the German capitulation in Berlin, and General Leclerc played the same role in the Bay of Tokyo on 15th September 1945. Finally, France took part in the construction of the UNO in San Francisco and inherited a permanent seat on the Security Council.

The General did not neglect the colonial problems which played a part in the rebirth of France. In January 1944, at Brazzaville, he had announced

De Gaulle and Molotov meet in Moscow, December 1944

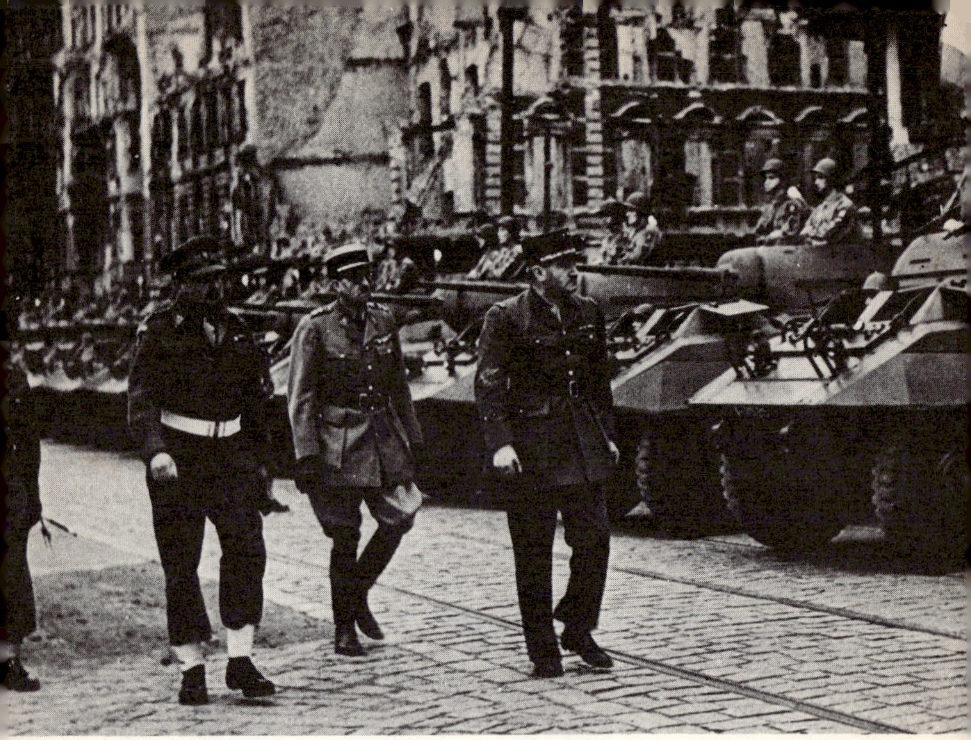

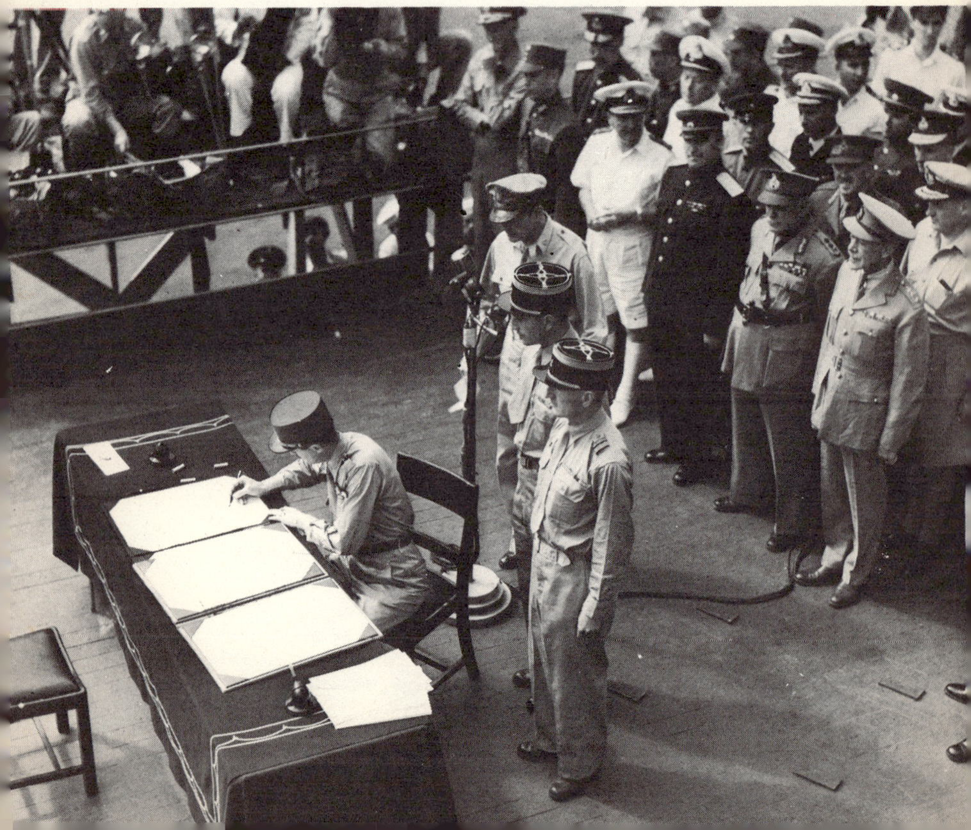

General Chaudasne inspects French armoured units following the fall of Berlin

that the Empire would become the *French Union* and declared that France was leading into a new era 62,000,000 people henceforth joined by her 42,000,000 children.' It was certainly a rather vague statement which probably did not take sufficient account of the growth of nationalism encouraged by the defeat of 1940, the decline of Europe, and the rise of the United States and the USSR. The cancer which was to gnaw at French politics for more than fifteen years had already begun.

On the very day of the German capitulation, grave disturbances broke out in Eastern Algeria. Their suppression resulted in several thousand deaths. In the Levant, the 'misunderstanding' persisted. France certainly intended to grant the independence offered in 1941, but accompanied by a triple convention – military, economic and cultural. An uprising broke out in Syria in May 1945

General Leclerc signs the Instrument of Japanese Surrender, September 1945

and was quickly put down. But the affair gave Great Britain the chance to strengthen her position in the Middle East. As a result, there was increased tension between Great Britain and France and a final confrontation between de Gaulle and Churchill. De Gaulle was not likely to forget it. The General summoned the British Ambassador on 4th June, told him to sit down and said: 'I realize that we are not at present in a position to declare war on you. But you have insulted and betrayed the West. We shall not forget it.'

Finally, France got back Indo-China, with relative ease in the south, thanks to the support of Lord Louis Mountbatten, but a great deal of difficulty in the Chinese-occupied north. Incidents in Hanoi and Saigon proved that the 'French presence' would be in jeopardy from then on.

Now that the guns were quiet, the main problem which faced de Gaulle was that of the political future of France. With the return of the prisoners of war, demobilization, and reversion to a more or less normal way of life, the Provisional Government and the Consultative Assembly, even though their ranks had been swelled since the Liberation, had reached the end of the road. The French people had to elect an assembly responsible for planning a new constitution. For the General, since the 'choice' of 1943, the problem was fundamental. The Fourth Republic had to divorce itself from sterile party struggles and escape impotence. There had to be a complete break between the Legislative and the Executive. His own preferences were for an American-style constitution with a president at its head.

On 24th October 1945, the French people were called to answer two questions in a referendum. Did they want a new constitution or a return

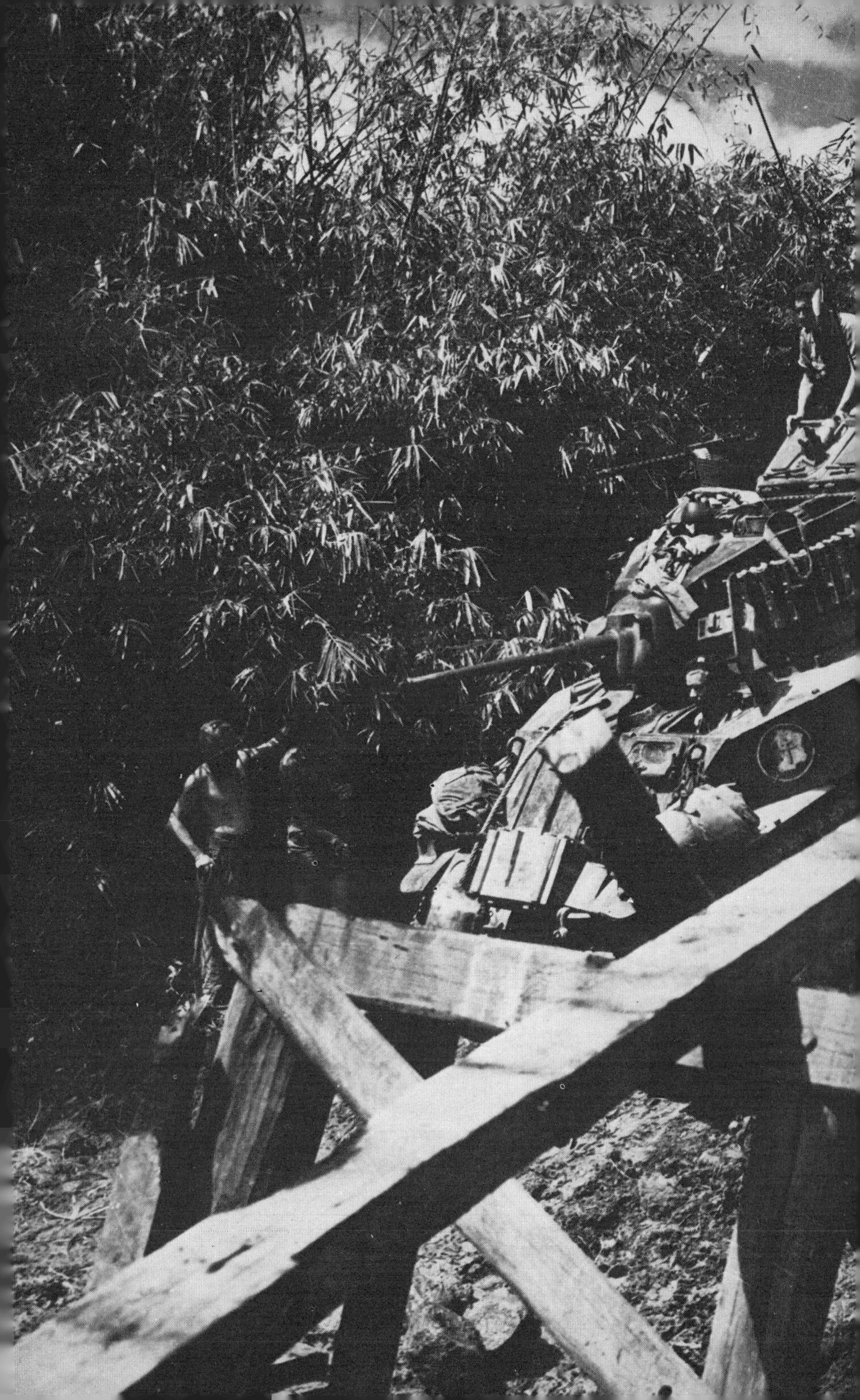

French troops in Indo-China

Leclerc with Ho Chi Minh, soon to prove an irremovable thorn in the side of his wartime allies

to that of 1875? Secondly, did they agree that the future assembly would have limited powers during the first thirty months when it would devote itself to drawing up the new constitution, and voting budgets, treaties and major reforms, thus leaving greater freedom of action to the government? The results seemed to confirm the General's wishes. The first 'yes' was by ninety-six per cent of the votes and the second by sixty-six per cent (the communists launched a campaign for the 'no'). But the victory was not complete. The elections took place on the same day as the referendum. They seemed to point to a desire for renewal. The old formations of the Right were crushed and the old radical party, bastion of the Third Republic, retained only 1,000,000 supporters. Three formations emerged from this disaster: the MRP (Popular Republican Movement, ex-social democrats) with almost twenty-three per cent of the votes, the Socialists with twenty-four per cent and the biggest surprise, the Communists with twenty-five per cent of the votes and 150 seats. They had won 5,000,000 votes against less than 1,500,000 in 1936.

How was the new Government to be formed? Leon Blum did not want an exclusively Socialist-Communist alliance any more than one with the MRP. Finally, the communists agreed to a 'tripartie' combination and on 13th November, General de Gaulle was unanimously elected head of government. But now that the war was over, the communists intended to occupy a key position. They demanded one of the three great ministries: Foreign Affairs, National Defence, or Interior. De Gaulle categorically opposed them and declared on the radio that he would refuse to 'entrust them with any of the three levers which control foreign policy, the diplomacy which expresses it,

Leclerc with Prince Sihanouk of Cambodia

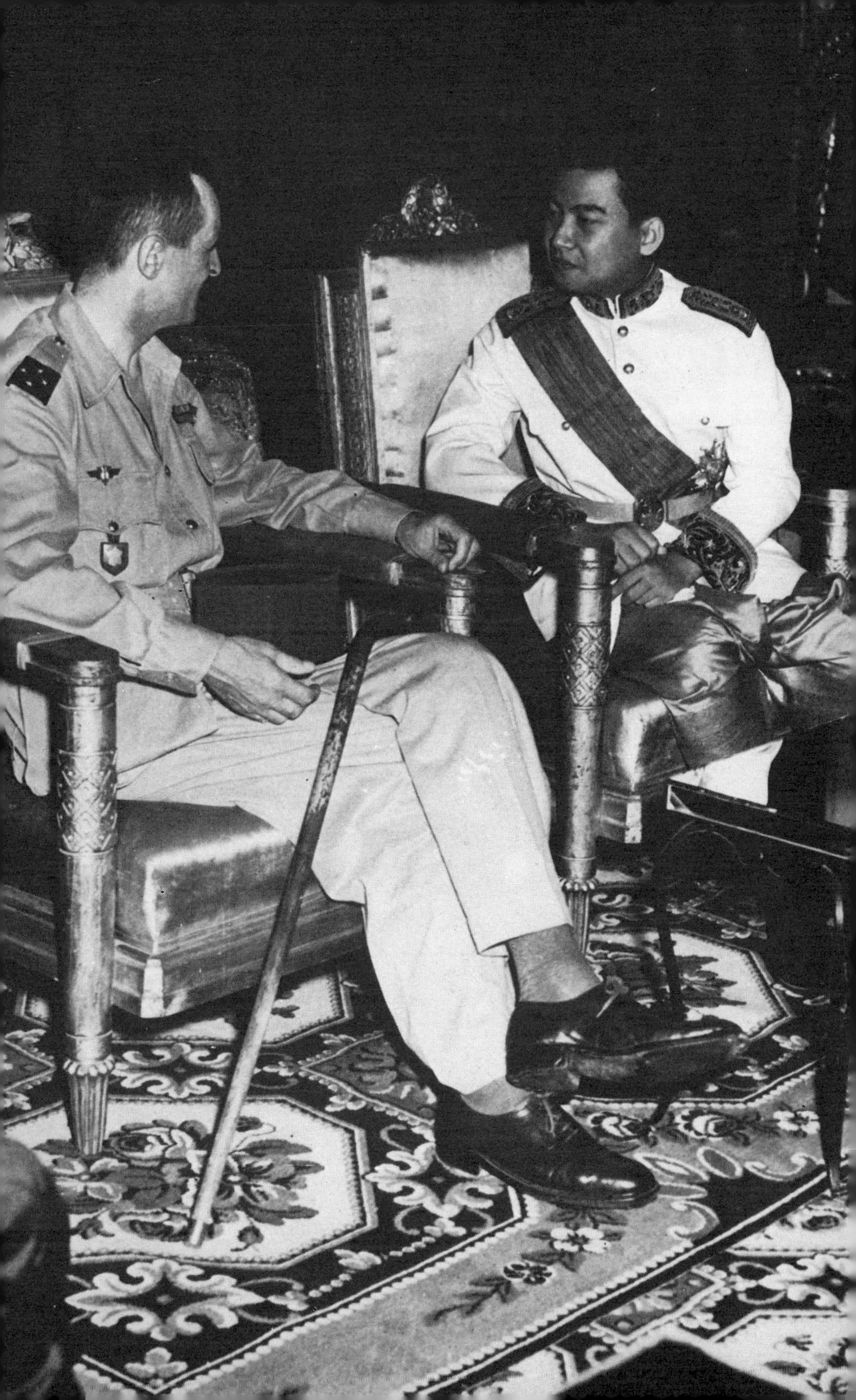

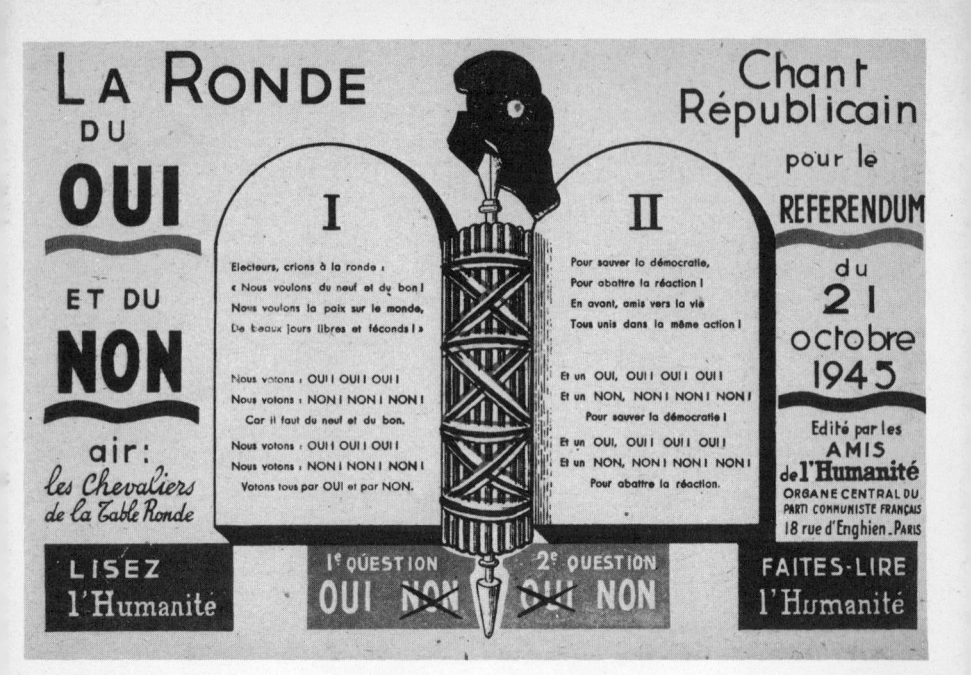

A Communist Party leaflet published during the Referendum of 24th October 1945

the army which upholds it, or the police who protect it.' It was a nice turn of phrase but it concealed a tactical withdrawal since the communists in fact obtained five portfolios. Tillon became Minister of Munitions; and, most important, Thorez became Vice-President of the Council.

This first contest proved that party politics had reappeared on the scene, to de Gaulle's intense annoyance, and the following weeks brought further proof. The conflict continued with the Socialists who were threatening a strike of the civil servants, and who, through their spokesman, André Philip, a Companion of the Liberation, asked for a reduction of twenty per cent in military supplies. For the General this was an inadmissible encroachment on forbidden ground. The Assembly was acting in excess of its rights. Finally, there was a supreme insult: the Assembly expressed its desire that the General should 'mind his own business'.

On 1st January 1946, de Gaulle underlined in Parliament the 'fundamental differences of opinion' which separated the government and the assembly. And he added: 'This is doubtless the last time that I shall speak in these precincts.' The next day he left for the South of France and 'meditated by the sea'. He returned to Paris on the 14th. The *coup de théâtre* came on Sunday the 20th. The General summoned his ministers to the Ministry of War, in the old room denuded of its armour. At midday he made his entry in uniform: 'The party system has reappeared in its totality. I cannot approve of it. But, other than using force to establish a dictatorship which I do not want and which would undoubtedly turn out badly, I can do nothing to stop it. I must therefore step down.'

So sudden a departure naturally caused amazement on all sides and a flood of editorial comment in the national press.

But in the country itself there was

a total lack of reaction. Not one strike, not one demonstration. When Léon Blum returned from captivity he said: 'Since I first set my foot on French soil again a week ago, I must admit that I have been filled with disappointment and foreboding because of this. I have not found what I expected . . . I do not feel that France has retutned to normal life. I do not feel that any function of the country has returned to normal.

'I see a sort of worn out convalescence, listless and lazy, which is the breeding ground for every sort of infection. With all our might we must fight against it, correct it, rectify it.'

It is true that the French, as soon as the theatre of the Liberation had closed its doors, began to worry again about the same mundane problems that had monopolized their attention for five years: food, heating, the black market. The end of the occupation did not bring any relief. The winter of 1944-45, with the disorganization of transport and the slump in production, was the worst of the war. A year later, there was still food rationing and it was necessary to reintroduce bread cards. The war and the occupation had also aggravated social jealousy. The peasants were the main beneficiaries of the black market, while the workers suffered by far the most, affected by the pay freeze, and by forced labour. Since the Liberation they had been suffering more than anyone else from the inflationary spiral. De Gaulle had blundered on this point. Refusing to 'overthrow the substance of the sick and wounded country', he had refused the Draconian monetary reforms proposed by Mendès France, following the example of Belgium. But despite considerable increases, wages did not succeed in matching prices and the standard of living in working class families remained very low.

The middle classes did not commit themselves on the subject of de Gaulle but basically they regarded him as a rampart against communism. The bourgeoisie was concerned about the social reforms which had been announced; couched in showy terms, they were in fact very limited in scope. De Gaulle had taken up the CNR's programme and set about the nationalization of the main public services, gas, electricity, etc, the coal industry, and the banks. At the same time he announced the creation of committees on industry and social security.

The purge, which was considered excessive by some and insufficient by others, was another bone of contention. Above all, this affected the ruling classes who had not spared their support for Pétain. It was true that it too often took on an arbitrary air, with its special tribunals and its juries composed entirely of members of the Resistance. The punishments, very severe at the beginning, became more lenient with time. Certain notorious collaborators or informers escaped proceedings, while the author Paul Chack was condemned to death and executed for having set up an anti-Bolshevik committee. Finally, it was not without a certain pang that many French people attended the trial of the Marshal. The investigation of his case was hasty, and no official documents whatsoever were produced. The Laval trial was sadly reminiscent of certain notorious aspects of totalitarian countries.

At her liberation, France succumbed to the charm of the charismatic leader, but she was quickly disenchanted. In fact, from 1944, de Gaulle appeared to be out of phase with the mass of the country. France saw de Gaulle as the man for dealing with storms, with hopeless cases, but unsuited to, or rather tiresome and even anachronistic in normal times. After the demonstration of the power of the German war machine and above all of American power, the country felt that France was nothing more than a second-rate power and they resigned themselves, too easily perhaps. Deep down the people were

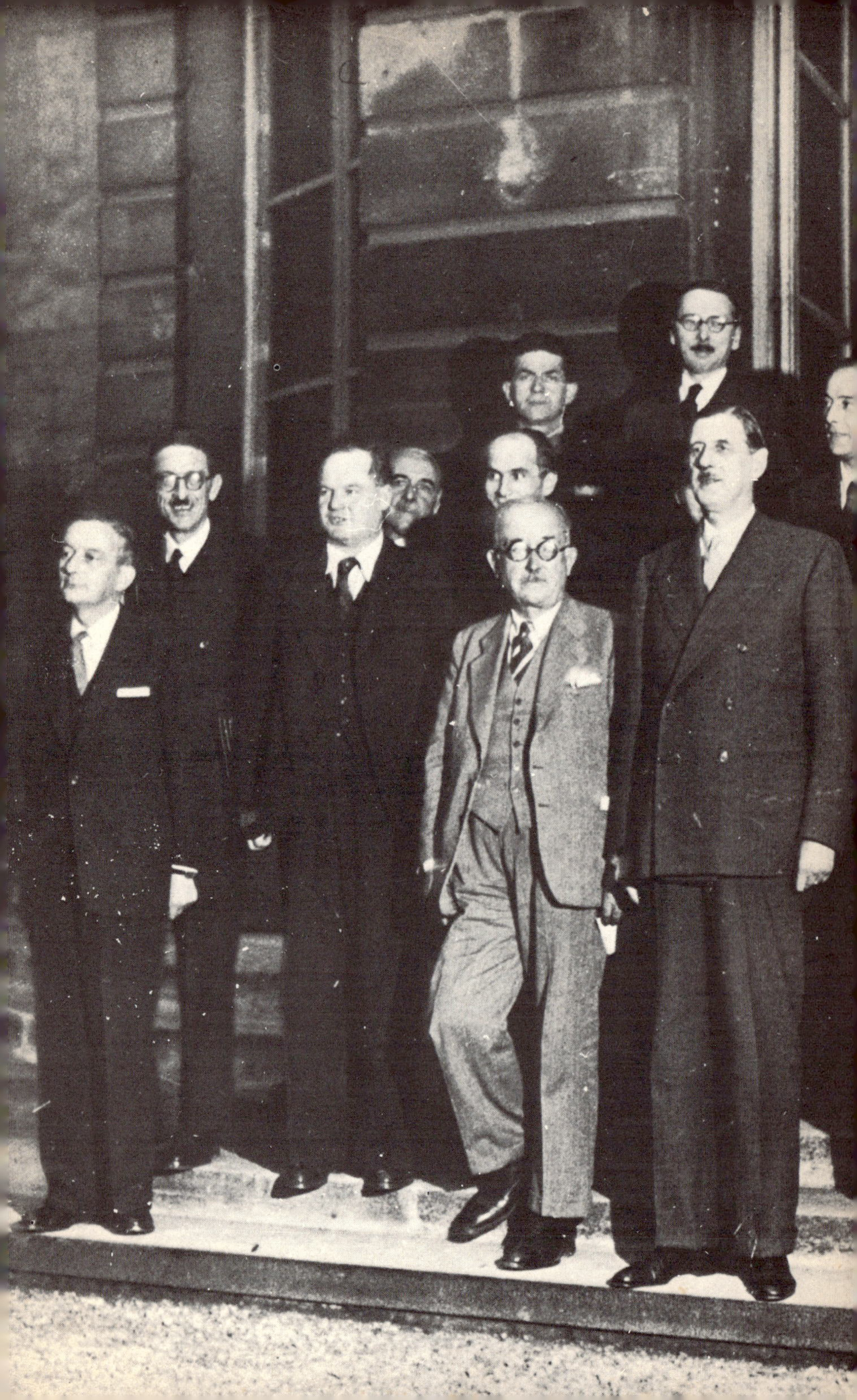

De Gaulle and his new government

weary. The war and the games of diplomacy irritated them. Their preoccupations turned towards economic and social matters. When they let de Gaulle go, the French people displayed the same reaction as the British people sacrificing Churchill to Attlee several months later. Besides, de Gaulle was aware of this situation: 'I tell you, administration is mean, petty, vexatious. Government is arduous, difficult, delicate. War, you see, war is horrifying, but peace, peace, it must be said, is tedious.'

The recognition of the parties also posed a difficult problem. But all the resistance movements had shown a desire for regeneration and a desire not to return to the institutions of the Third Republic and the sterile games of the inter-war period. The purge itself, which had eliminated, one way or another, most of the former political groupings, seemed to guarantee this desire for renewal. But in November 1945 there was a rebirth of political pluralism, a rise of actions, and the Assembly gave birth to a constitution which differed little from that of 1875. There is no one exaplanation for this. It seems that four years of tribulation could not rid the French of their old habits. Furthermore, the purge had spared the oldtimers of politics like Herriot and Blum for whom loyalty to the party came before the general interest. Finally, the new political chess board already implied a sterile strategy. The socialist party did not want an alliance with the communists and spent its time trying to outbid them while retaining its distance from the great party of the centre, the MRP. There was no possibility of a stable majority.

De Gaulle had already considered an appeal to the people when he was in Algiers. But, in spite of his public speeches and the positions he adopted on the radio, the unanimous support he expected was not forthcoming. On this point, the General had made an error of judgement. He had mistaken the crowds who were eager to answer his call for the masses. Far from being the mass of the population, his supporters were not in the majority. In fact they were scarcely a quarter, mostly those who had voted for the MRP. De Gaulle found himself out on a limb. His desire for national independence and his strong sense of the State should have gained him the support of the traditional Right Wing. But he had been separated from them ever since 1940. Many conservatives saw in the fall of France, only a 'divine intervention', the collapse of a discredited régime, and they hastened to join the 'national revolution' of Vichy. De Gaulle is supposed to have said in London: 'I had hoped that the leaders of the administrations, the churches, the general staff would come and join me . . . Instead I saw arrive the unfortunate, the unimportant.' One of his colleagues said of the Free French, 'c'est le métro'.

Paradoxically, it was the Left, pacifist by nature, which rallied to the champion of French greatness, out of hatred for totalitarianism or because of the force of circumstances, like the communists. The restoration of peace, fear of authoritarian power, the primacy of social questions brought about a divorce between de Gaulle and most of his 'fellow travellers'.

The last question concerns the actual departure of the General. Was it a manoeuvre or final retirement? In his *Mémoires*, de Gaulle admits that he was tempted to resort to a military coup d'état with Leclerc's troops. It seems that he recoiled from the risks of a dictatorship. In fact, the explanation probably does not lie there. On 20th January 1946, de Gaulle was convinced that he would be recalled within six months. His departure was one more poker bluff, a 'mishap' he declared to his friend Rémy Roure. The impotence of the

The punishment of a collaborator

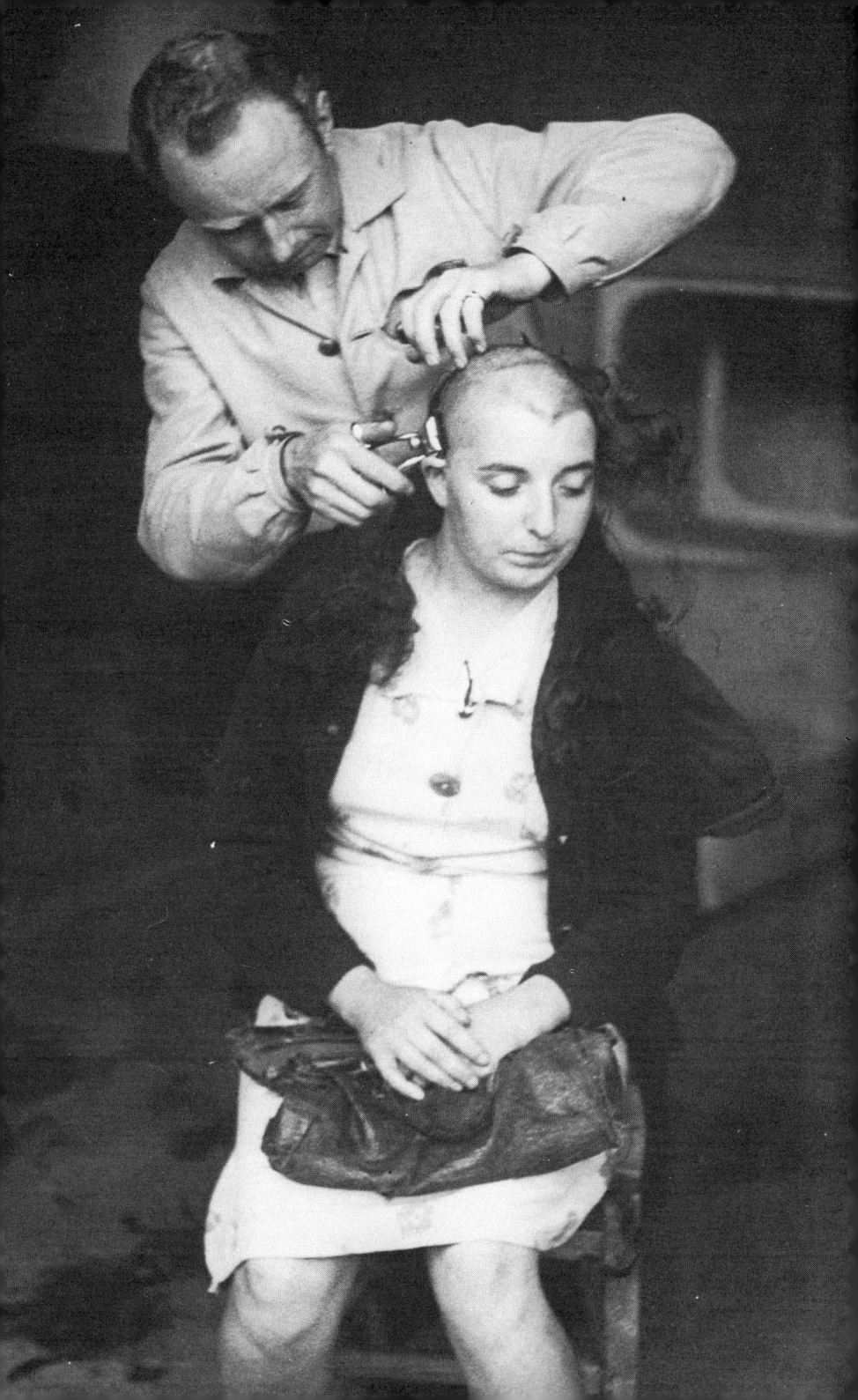

parties would oblige them to call upon him sooner or later. In fact, the 'journey in the desert' was to last twelve years.

The scene on 16th January marked the end of the first act of a public life. This departure, which was not 'lacking in grandeur' in the words of Thorez, naturally gave rise to impassioned discussion concerning both the man of 18th June and the head of the government.

At first glance, the balance sheet of the actions of the leader of the Free French seems to defy criticism. But it has been argued, and not without reason, that a French Resistance would have been born anyway, without the call from London. The phenomenon arose from the state of Europe and was natural in a total war of an ideological nature. Sooner or later this resistance would have had a leader. Men like Muselier, Giraud, and above all, Catroux, less intransigent, less touchy, more flexible, and more diplomatic would probably have been better defenders of France's cause and have reaped greater advantages from the Allies.

But it is no less true that the role of General de Gaulle was of capital importance and that he was probably the only man capable of giving a passionate and genuine image of a France struck down by defeat. The very weakness of his resources made it possible, with his intransigence and his refusal of all 'temporary expedients', for him to embody the political conscience of the Allies and to become in some way the symbol of the resistance of the free world against Hitler's tyranny. It was a tour de force. Despite his derisory resources, de Gaulle managed to burn himself into people's minds, on a level with those who had power and force: Churchill, Roosevelt, Eisenhower . . .

De Gaulle's actions as head of government have also been the subject of bitter polemics. There again the balance sheet seems in credit at first glance. Did not General de Gaulle re-establish the State, avoid both civil war and communist dictatorship, and give France back her place among the great nations of the world? But some would reproach him for having forgotten the cardinal virtue of the Prince, clemency. They would accuse him of having re-established domestic peace at the price of exorbitant concessions to the communists. Besides there was little chance of the communists bringing off a take-over in Western Europe at the time. The example of Italy, whose political climate and conditions are not unlike those of France, have shown this to be true.

Others maintain that France had merely returned to a place of secondary importance in the world which, because of her demographic and economic potential, she would have regained anyway. They have reproached the General for having a passion, too exclusive and too abstract, for France as symbolized by 'Madonna of the fresco', to the detriment of the real France, battered and suffering.

All these critics have forceful arguments. But the fact remains that de Gaulle proved himself the jealous guardian of the collective destiny of the Nation and he showed unswerving devotion to the State. His voluntary retirement to lofty solitude placed him above private interests, put him in reserve, made him the vigilant sentinel of the country's future and gave him the possibility of one day rendering France 'a signal service'.

Despite his shortcomings, his mistakes, even his faults, his was a prodigious personal adventure; he was a man apart, capable of provoking both hatred and passion, but whose bearing, exaggerated in everything, defied ordinary rules.

Place de la Concorde. De Gaulle presents flags to the reconstituted regiments of the French army

Bibliography

An Explanation of De Gaulle by Robert Aron (Harper and Row, New York)
Crusade in Europe by Dwight D Eisenhower (Doubleday, New York)
De Gaulle by Alexander Werth (Penguin Books, London and New York)
De Gaulle entre deux mondes by J M de la Groce (Paris 1964)
Diplomat Among Warriors by R D Murphy (Collins, London. Doubleday, New York)
Envers et contre tous by J Soustelle (Paris 1950)
Pétain et de Gaulle by J R Tournoux (Paris 1964)
Resistance Versus Vichy by Peter Novick (Chatto and Windus, London. Columbia University Press, New York)
Seeds of Discord by D S White (Syracuse University Press, New York)
The Complete War Memoirs of Charles de Gaulle by General C de Gaulle (Simon and Schuster, New York)